ULTIMATE WONDER PLANTS

YOUR URBAN JUNGLE INTERIOR

IRENE SCHAMPAERT & JUDITH BAEHNER

Lannoo

FOREWORD

We believe you can find a good place for plants in every interior. Some living greenery in our home is something we can no longer do without, it's not too bold to say that green is the new black. Because green is here to stay. Green is the ultimate interior hero. Green is at the heart of our busy homes, a calm point in our all-too-hectic schedules. It makes us think, look, stand still by the beauty and ultimate force that is mother nature. More green, growing plants in our homes - that's what we want for our own home and yours as well. Green is present in every part of our lives. We read about it in interior design magazines, see flowers and plants in stores, restaurants and cafés. Plants are good for us; they inspire daydreams of nature and add colour to our interiors, and they literally make us healthier because plants purify our air.

Whether you live in the northern or southern hemisphere, whether your house is more minimal in style, bohemian, eclectic or has sleek, modern lines, whether you live in a big house with huge windows or a cosy, compact studio, every interior can incorporate a dash of green. As with many things in life, it's about making the right choices and we are here to help you with your green choices.

Ultimate Wonderplants brings back the most exquisite green interiors from *Wonderplants* and *Wonderplants 2*. We have selected twenty-five ultimate green interiors, that will make you want to create your own green jungle.

We aim to inspire you, share our passion for plants, show you which plants do best in different locations, which will flourish in a dark corner and which will brighten up your bathroom. This book tells you how to create and care for your urban jungle. In *Ultimate Wonderplants* we want to encourage you to follow your intuition in your own style with plants that you find beautiful so you can decide whether you opt for a subtle approach or prefer to go all the way. This book provides you with lots of information about the best plants to choose, how to care for your plants and what plants can do for you and your environment. We're delighted to share our passion for fantastic interiors and plants, each with its own story and each beautifully unique.

Irene and Judith

CONTENT

WABI-SABI

STOCKHOLM SE

Fresh green plants and bare wood in a hushed colour palette. This house in Östermalm, one of the more central districts in Stockholm, was inspired by Japanese style and exudes serenity. Johanna Welander and Per Holmqvist, both architects, were very passionate about the raw structure of the building, but in particular saw the potential to transform it into a tranquil, open place.

Concrete floors, concrete walls, concrete ceilings. This house in Stockholm is in true *wabi-sabi* style. When the owner of this imposing building in Östermalm, in the heart of Stockholm, decided to make various rooms available for people to lease and buy, Johanna Welander and Per Holmqvist did not hesitate for one second. The basement would be theirs. The dilapidated ceiling was replaced by a concrete structure, and sufficient light was drawn into the interior. A few square metres were sacrificed to create a small, private garden, which also had a huge impact on the interior and created a welcoming outdoor feeling.

Although the rough, grey stone may form the distinctive basis, the overall design looks anything but cold. Natural materials such as wood and terracotta as well as strategically placed plants–specifically plants with patterned leaves–set the tone in this Japanese-inspired interior. The residents deliberately opted for second-hand furniture and reusable materials, as it gave them substantial quality at a relatively low price. Subtle art on the wall and rural still-life paintings provide the interior design with a very distinctive style.

CINEMA FLORA

CREMONA IT

"A rare opportunity, a place with potential, but above all, love at first sight." That's how Attilio Solzi and Paola Galli described this old cinema they found during their search for a home in northwest Italy, in Lombardy. Their amazement was complete when they entered the building, surrounded by old farms.

It was a soaring space awash in light. Countless elements worth keeping, and a wide range of options for dividing the space in original and imaginative ways. The conversion from a former cinema into a functional residence became a renovation process seeking a beautiful balance between the old and the new. The maroon curtains are still there, although they are now part of the kitchen, while the orange sign above the entrance has become the name plate. Several lovely design objects have been added to the interior, with a humoristic note here and there.

What was once the theatre is now the living room. The 'lounge loft', as they now call the open space under the roof, is the relaxation area, as well as the spot where the plants in this house are kept: concentrated in a few square metres, with a huge impact on the rest of the house. The large Swiss cheese plant is partly responsible for that, as is the fiddle-leaf fig, which often grows to a tremendous size. They combine beautifully with the hanging plant which has been draped on the entresol, with ample room to grow.

GREEN, GREY & GLAMOROUS

ANTWERP BE

Right in the heart of the Antwerp Diamond Quarter is the home of an architect with a green thumb. His spacious triplex house was renovated extensively by Dirk Engelen, who respected what was already there. The lusciously thriving greenery softens the atmosphere of the prevalently present concrete. A paragon of urban glamour.

The Jerusalem of the North is what people sometimes call the district at the edge of Antwerp's City Park. The strong presence of the Orthodox Jewish community, together with the local diamond traders, gives this district an idiosyncratic and pleasant ambiance. "It is a fascinating environment," according to Dirk Engelen, founder and practicing architect at B-architecten. "There is a wonderful mix of cultures here, with schools next to synagogues in the same street, and I experience a kind of friendly aloofness here which I greatly appreciate. This is a very pleasant place to live."

In a street lined with rows of plane trees, Dirk bought a building from the 1970s over nine years ago, and he currently lives on the top three floors. "It was originally an office building of the Health Insurance Fund," Dirk says, "completely built in concrete, with a boxy, unimaginative structure and a balcony on each floor." The plan? To create his own world behind that grey wall, to infuse it with a completely new, vibrant feel while utilising and emphasising the original qualities of the building. Objective achieved: the core of the building was opened up, its spaciousness restored.

"The house had been renovated at an earlier stage, some time in the 1980s," Dirk relates, "including suspended ceilings. The building became congested. But behind that renovation, we discovered the beautiful original concrete ceiling, which we restored to its previous glory; that eventually defined the essence of the current dwelling. We have extended its former grandeur, but in a contemporary way. With big open spaces and new stairs within the home."

Quite early in the renovation process, it became clear that the abundance of nature really had to have an important place, and for several reasons.

"From an architectural point of view, I thought it was interesting to extend the green environment which we live in into the building," says Dirk. "Ecological considerations also played a role, because plants add peace and quiet in an indoor environment."

Dirk specifically took into account the huge Swiss cheese plant that he had grown in his former residence, which would receive a prominent place in the living room after this renovation. What was then a three-year old specimen has by now grown so big that it extends into the space above, and is responsible for that touch of glamour in the formerly brutish interior.

On the ground floor of the triplex residence, the architect installed a huge planter where the sentry plant constitutes a subtle, yet important part of the kitchen, with its white, concrete-poured flooring and concrete kitchen island. In addition, there is the patio that provides plenty of space for outdoor plants, preferably plants that require little pruning. And finally, there is the green roof, which also relies on significant support from the City of Antwerp. It not only provides solid insulation, it also benefits public health and the environment – and is also a very beautiful solution.

A win-win situation, according to Dirk. "The multitude and variety of plants have a soothing effect, and maintaining them is sheer relaxation to me. That way I can sustain everything with relative ease and a great deal of fun."

ASIAN DREAM
CHAU DOC VN

There is efficiency galore in this co-housing project in Chau Doc, a city close to the Mekong river in the southern part of Vietnam. Despite the limitations enforced by local legislation, Nishizawa Architects succeeded in erecting a contemporary building with some extraordinary features. This residence, built from wood and rotating corrugated metal sheets, benefits from natural ventilation and is suffused with light. It has room for three families as well as a veritable indoor jungle.

The original building, an old wooden house with terracotta roof tiles, was converted into a residence with corrugated steel sheets. The sheets are a popular building material in the region because they do not cost much and make it possible to build a house within a very short time frame. The architecture firm of Shunri Nishizawa not only had to take into account the rainy season and the fragile soil quality in the area, but local building regulations as well. Their design perfectly fulfilled the requirements of the residents.

The house accommodates three couples and their respective children. They share one communal living area, with rotating corrugated metal sheets providing that lovely outdoor feeling. The sheets engage the residence with the layered landscape–floating houses, built on a raft made of empty oil barrels; traditional stilt houses; the abundance of rice fields, ...

The timber-frame construction with its suspended floors is responsible for the warm and intimate atmosphere in the house, giving the architect the option to create separate rooms for the residents. The abundance of sunlight and the open spaces not only allow tropical and other plants to grow in the residence, but trees as well, here and there rising right through the suspended floors. That extraordinary amount of greenery in the house is a given for the residents; each of them grew up in an environment where time and space were spent on indoor and outdoor plants. Maintaining the greenery is a daily ritual.

The choice of plants in the communal living area happened by mutual consultation. It was a unanimous decision that the lovely, fragrant jasmine and small-leaved plane, an exotic bush with bracts of yellow flowers, red flyleaves and black fruits, should be present in abundance. These plants, some of which are over ten years old, make strong statements.

PARIS TEXAS

ANTWERP BE

She's a Parisian architect; he's a Texan artist. Nathalie Wolberg and Tim Stokes live and work together in a building in Antwerp that they named Paris Texas, situated in the notorious maritime district, around the corner from the imposing Museum Aan de Stroom. They each have their own studio in the building and provide short-term rentals for photoshoots and pop-up shops. This building also harbours a vibrant life between colourful walls in hidden corners, and under bright neon lights, but most of all, living greenery. The border between interior and exterior is almost confusingly blurred.

The decision to relocate to Antwerp was easy for these two. "We were absolutely smitten by the energy and creativity that the city exudes," Nathalie smiles. The building had housed an import-export business for years and was in dire need of thorough renovations. The original structure was kept largely intact, transformed into a modular environment where light, colour and texture define the atmosphere in the various rooms. The building now combines an exhibition hall, three studios, the kitchen as a communal area, a library, a guest room and an apartment on the first floor.

Without a doubt, the heart of Paris Texas is the garden. "I had been dreaming for years of a garden in an exotic style," Nathalie says. Landscape architects Bart and Pieter made her dream come true, with flair and panache. The mustard-yellow colour

of the garden wall underlines that tropical feeling.

Nathalie has always loved spending time in nature, wild and exotic, preferably as close to a jungle as possible. Less enchanted by houseplants, she decided to integrate a sort of garden into the heart of the home, incorporating trees and outdoor plants and reserving a striking spot for the incredibly huge dragon tree, which has been planted rather than potted. Tim's studio is home to numerous cacti, succulents and other plants that peep out between the artworks. In the apartment, the greenery almost becomes a graphic element against the pastel pink backdrop.

Tim's interest in plants developed gradually. His passion for plants began when he started helping Nathalie care for the plants in their home. Nathalie primarily focuses on taking care of the garden, which offers a gorgeous décor.

OFICIO STUDIO

MADRID ES

In the heart of Madrid, in the middle of the triangle known as
Paseo del Arte, stands a building that has been there for centuries.
Neglected for years, it has received a new lease on life from
Melina Carranza and David Iglesias. The two now live and work
there together, accompanied by their dog and surrounded by a
striking assortment of plants.

Right time, right place. That's what happened to Melina from Mexico when she dropped by David's bicycle shop to get her bike fixed during her holiday in Madrid. They ended up talking mainly about their shared passion for fine leather goods, since her lovely handbag had not escaped his keen eye for detail. The ice was broken; the rest is history.

Some time later, they moved into a house in the Barrio de las Letras neighbourhood, in the shade of the Prado museum and several other prestigious historic monuments. The previous owner had used the building as storage space for over ten years, doing virtually no maintenance in the meantime. They stumbled across unique finds, but above all the place was deep-cleaned. The artistic duo currently lives and works in what is now known as Oficio Studio. At this location, fine leather goods are produced and customers are welcomed.

The move from a subtropical region in Mexico to downtown Madrid was quite an adjustment for the lady of the house. She was unaccustomed to adapting to the changing seasons. The sense of being constantly surrounded by gorgeous nature in full bloom was sorely missed. Over the years, she assembled a lovely collection of plants. The building, which receives a great deal of indirect light thanks to the large windows and direct sunlight here and there and with its soaring four-metre ceilings, was the perfect place to display her beautiful collection. It also softened the building's intrinsic industrial look.

A corner in the studio was selected to place a large assortment of plants in a cluster, creating the impression of a garden inside the house. The 'indoor jungle' that it has become by now is tended with great love and attention. The plants are strategically positioned and structured according to the care they need.

The Swiss cheese plant has a prominent spot in the kitchen, as it's the couple's favourite; they also cultivate plants that add a Mexican note to Melina's culinary delights.

GREEN
DIY DREAM

MELBOURNE AU

Handmade carpets, self-designed furniture and designer items from the 1950s. Warm, soft colours alongside natural hues and materials. Finally, a less than obvious collection of plants, in pots that they designed personally. Warmth and personality galore in this country manor near Melbourne. To Poppy and Scott, it is the house of their dreams.

Show me how you live and I will tell you who you are." Your interior is an extension of your personality. This sentiment is old hat to the residents of this special house, built in the 1970s. The story of Poppy Lane and Scott Gibson almost seems like a fairy-tale. She is a florist and he is a craftsman. Under the name Pop & Scott, they design furniture, household items and a very popular collection of painted pots. They successfully run a workshop and showroom in Northcote.

Together with their two children, they live in Elthow, a green suburb of Melbourne. The couple rents the house, so renovations were not an option. They did spend considerable time and energy on decorating and upgrading the garden. "I want my interior to tell my own story; I want to put a piece of myself into it," Poppy tells us. "When decorating, I run by my intuition. I love every single piece in this house, and that is essential," she believes.

The house is home to many of their own creations: the handwoven lampshades, the carpets, and the many plaster pots with their characteristic warm colours, understated shapes and graphic patterns.

Morevoer, the latter serve their purpose. Each room of the house has plants, most of them sizable specimens. "I have not known any other life," Poppy reminisces. "My mother was a florist and born with a green thumb. In a very natural way and with tremendous finesse, she cared for the greenery in the house and kept the garden. I cannot imagine a life without them."

The right plant is in the right pot in the right room. Poppy was meticulous in her choices of all the greenery. The living area has plants with flowers in fresh colours, which is reflected in the choice of decoration and textiles, while plants with less pronounced shapes and colours are in the bedroom. "A plant can intensify the mood of a certain room, and that is a challenge," says Poppy. "The best example is the *Philodendron martianum* on the table in the dining room," she ventures.

With growing children in the house, the interest in air-purifying plants has also grown, and she now only buys plants that come with care instructions. "You need to be aware of how to care for them," she says. "Only then will it become a relaxing pastime and the rest will come naturally."

ISAAC WALLIN

SCANDINAVIAN IMMACULACY

COPENHAGEN DK

The luxuriant orangery, tended with loving care for thirty years by the previous owner, helped this house in Frederiksberg, a prime neighbourhood in Copenhagen, bring its new owner closer to nature. In some sense, Danish interior stylist Rikke Graff Juel saw it as a sacred duty to carry on this long labour of love, gradually embracing the passion for plants that can now be felt throughout the house.

Summer had already drawn to a close when Rikke and her husband and two children moved into this house, which is an excellent example of Functionalist architecture. Right from the start, they had to figure out how to help the plants in the orangery – which she herself calls 'the heart of the household' – survive the winter. "Spring revealed what a gorgeous green oasis this spot harbours," Rikke says.

As the years passed, green tendrils crept into the rest of the house, adding lush notes to the blond Scandinavian interior. Rikke enjoys grouping the plants. "When you achieve the right combination, it has the most spectacular botanical impression," she explains. The bright green leaves of the dwarf banana tree contrast with greyish-green shades like the elephant's ear. Large alongside small, stylised and neat alongside exuberant and overgrown.

Inspired by Mediterranean-style homes, several walls in the house were given a deep green shade. The colour choice of the rough, unpolished materials, like wood, reed and leather, incorporated into the interior only enhances the botanical impression.

The elephant's ear is Rikke's favourite plant by far. She adores the plant's beautifully sculptured shape and its woolly leaves. "I love the impression they give of having already lived a long life, like an elephant." she concludes.

FRENCH
GRANDEUR

PARIS FR

Around the corner from Parc Montsouris, in the artistic Quartier XIV
in Paris, Jean-Marc Dimanche had the house of his dreams built for him.
The modernist residence, inspired by the works of Le Corbusier, as with
many others in this district, includes an impressive, vertical courtyard
garden. It is the crowning glory of the interior, situated amongst a
sophisticated, idiosyncratic mix of vintage and design.

The last thing Jean-Marc had even dared to consider during his quest for a residence in the city was to have one built for himself, but that was exactly what happened. He has been living there with his wife and three children for about thirteen years now. The house is also the core of all his professional activities (Jean-Marc is an art director), with an agency on the ground floor and an exhibition space where artists can display their art privately and with ease.

Designed by the French firm XY Architecture, the residence was erected on a vacant lot between two buildings, and consists of seven storeys. Jean-Marc: "From the very beginning of the preparatory thought process, it had been the intention to utilise the building as completely as possible. That meant that we would not create a garden, but instead equip each floor with patios in order to get maximum enjoyment from the outdoor areas."

When the family moved from the countryside to Paris, Jean-Marc dreamt of a vertical courtyard garden. The desire to remain surrounded by nature was strong. "Bringing green into my environment was the only way for me to give nature its place in the city," Jean-Marc says. "It would be a waste to banish it from the buildings. I love the dialogue between the patios and the salon, extended, continuous nature."

Botanist and friend of the family Patrick Blanc, who is famous for his vertical gardens and being specialised in exotic plants, designed the wall of plants. "The wall in my house more closely resembles a jungle than a highly structured mosaic carpet," Jean-Marc continues. "Over the years, the plants have taken over the initiative and some versions have 'devoured' others. The current situation has strayed strongly from the plant chart Patrick had envisioned: it is almost as if nature practiced free expression here."

And, that is a fortunate coincidence, as this plant lover prefers the organic and spontaneous, and therefore also wild gardens.

"Let us say that I am more inclined to the lusciousness of English gardens than the symmetry and patterns of the French gardens," Jean-Marc concludes.

He takes us back to his childhood days to illustrate his passion for nature. "I believe I was six or seven years old when I started gardening. My mother's enthusiasm for gardens was contagious, to say the least," Jean-Marc reminisces. "I have been active in the garden-ing world for twenty years now. For instance, I helped organise the Plant Days in Courson from 1996 to 2016. It was there that I met and befriended many landscape architects and gardeners, amongst others Patrick Blanc. Besides being one of my passions, it has also become an important part of my life."

Jean-Marc was likewise as passionate about decorating the interior of his home. "It is safe to say that my interior is somewhat of a cabinet of curiosities; a mixture of designer items, old furniture and objects. I always trust my feeling. I first need to fall in love with a piece before I place it in my house," Jean-Marc confesses. "Each object tells its own story and is associated with some kind of encounter. Bringing all those different elements together and having them engage in dialogue: that is what intrigues me."

His biggest source of inspiration? Art and design guru Axel Vervoordt. "Because of his talent to reunite pieces of different origins and different periods, always respecting authenticity," Jean-Marc concludes. "Something that I continuously pursue myself as well."

GREEN
STATEMENTS

MILAN IT

Bright white walls, polished concrete, cast-iron constructions and statements incorporating plants. The ultimate basis for a glamorous interplay between structures and colour, volume and light. A former factory in Milan is now home and workplace to artist Antonino Sciortino, where he proudly showcases his own creations.

G limpsing the interior of Antonino Sciortino's home is a wonderful experience, since the artist himself has designed numerous artistic interiors. Even when he was just eight years old, he helped his father forge iron in the Palermo studio. His passion for dance brought him to Rome, where he spent his time shaping iron into design objects between choreography sessions, before moving to a former factory in a suburb of Milan. The house he lives and works in now is the perfect location to display his own work, a place where old and new design converge and greenery runs rampant. The green has an amazing impact in this interior against the backdrop of the pale, cool palette of colours and the iron structures. Some of the impressively tall cacti seem to have melded organically with the architecture. The massive aloe in the living room is over 100 years old; its immense bulk provides imposing balance.

INDOOR PATIO

AVARE BR

Designing a house without knowing whom shall live in it?
In the context of a real estate project, the architects at Studio
Vão designed three extraordinary houses for future residents.
Embracing a flexible structure and variations in the interior
spaces, they tried to provide room for families with different
natures. We took a peek inside 'The Ownerless House n°01'.

The red, slanted façade guides your eye to the starting point. In this building project, Studio Vão wants to make a statement. "By having open and closed rooms that alternate and are connected to each other, we can let the changing seasons play an important role in the living experience of the residents," according to the architects.

The team of experienced designers used the soft slope across the site to divide the residence into two levels: the social rooms on the one hand and the private rooms on the other. The kitchen and living room look out on a sunny patio, but have been specifically built around an indoor garden. Ultra-thin glass doors around the entire house blur the boundaries between outdoors and indoors. The stairs lead the traveller to the second level, which is where the bathroom and bedrooms have been placed.

A colourful tile floor with a patterned design creates the link between the patio and their 'indoor' version. Both have a pergola, made from a concrete grid. The technique is as simple as it is ingenious – and it's the trademark of Brazilian architect Rino Levi. It draws a maximum of natural daylight into the house. The tropical variety of plants in the indoor garden grows proliferously and in the best possible conditions.

However, the team also took into account the luscious vegetation on the façade. Due to the triangle-shaped openings in the roof, the front garden is also provided with the daylight it needs to flourish.

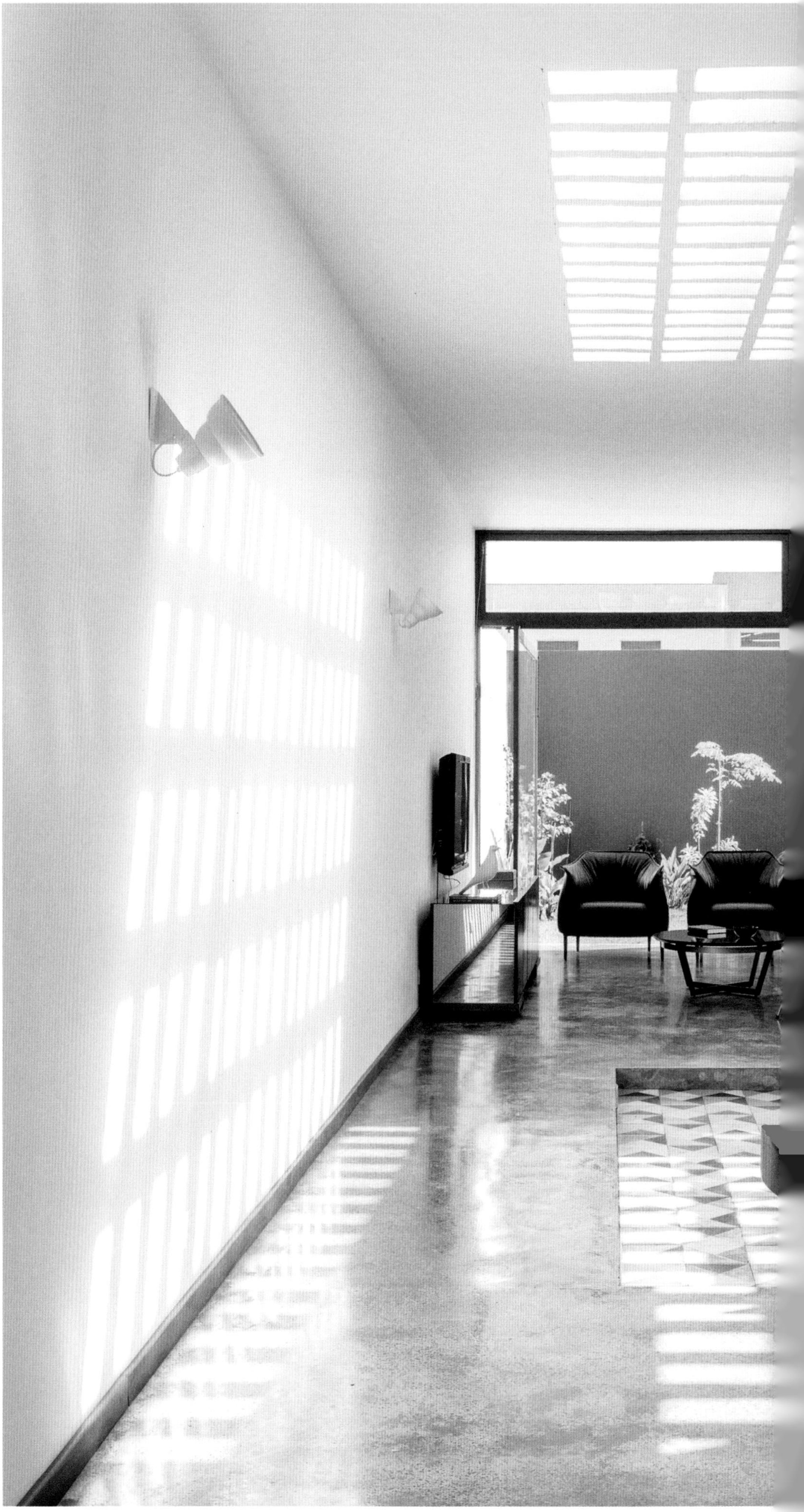

BOTANIC
ELEGANCE

GHENT BE

A few years ago, Jan and Daniël left their home in a former
renovated nursery school in Moustier and moved to Ghent,
the city where their florist shop Bluet is located. The house they
live in now, a protected historic building dating back to 1690,
had been on their radar for some time. The daily commute
began to take its toll; the city beckoned.

GThe house was originally a high-class town-
house with an elegant drawing room; its ro-
coco interior has been preserved beautifully.
The living room, once the salon of a man who
was most likely a merchant, still retains the
original Regency-style ceiling. When Jan and Daniël stripped
the wallpaper in the hallway to redo that area, they discovered
the Empire-era murals.

Daniël has been passionate about plants since the age of
twelve, a legacy handed down by his family. He headed off to
agricultural college at a young age and has been working pro-
fessionally with flowers and plants for over twenty years now. "I
love plants even more because I work with them so frequently,"

Daniël states. He occasionally ends up owning several unique items, due in no small part to the many connections he has established over the years. For instance, he has an exceptional collection of cacti in his store, compliments of a grower who is also a friend of his.

The many plants in their home are there for various reasons. "A home without plants is a house devoid of life," Daniël reasons. "But it's also a great way of testing which plants will flourish in various spots and it helps me figure out how to advise my customers, which is very important to me." Both of them also find it fascinating to focus on this passion in different ways. At home as a key element in the morning routine, and later in the day as a professional occupation.

Daniël's favourite plant is the prayer plant, because it seems to live out a more independent existence than other vegetation. It folds up its fascinating, colourful leaves beautifully every evening. The prayer plant in their home is absolutely huge.

PASTEL
PERFECT

LA US

Puno and Daniel were gifted the loft of their lives as if it were meant to be. At a unique location in downtown LA's Fashion District, they transformed a home previously occupied by friends into a living and working space with Scandinavian influences and tropical charm. And, they saw that it was good.

One good turn deserves another. When Puno and Daniel's best buddies moved house about two years ago, their gorgeous loft came on the market. "It was like a gift from heaven," Puno tells us enthusiastically. "We were looking for a house with enough space to work and live there, sufficient daylight in the house, and situated in a nice residential district, if we could somehow swing it. An opportunity such as this we could just not pass up on. It was by far the most beautiful loft we had visited."

Puno and her husband are particularly pleased with the neighbourhood they live in. "We are from a part of LA where everyone travels by car. I was so done with that. Here you can do everything on foot, or by bike, which enhances the connection with your living environment." The social aspect was the real deciding factor for them. "The optimism, the passion and creativity prevalent in this district has a huge impact on daily

life here. It makes the district vibrant," Puno tells us. "It is very easy to make contact with the creative scene here. I love the inpsiring input that it provides and gain a lot of energy from it."

Puno eagerly describes the interior of the loft as 'Scandi tropical'. It's a nice name for this loft with its sleek lines and shapes, the scattered echoes of pastel shades and the abundance of plants, often neatly grouped. The red sofa and some idiosyncratic designer items add character to the interior.

Their love of nature slowly grew. "Before we moved to LA, we lived in Venice in a house with a patio which was home to an extraordinary collection of luscious plants." Puno recalls the lovely scents from the jasmine, the passiflora with its gorgeous flow-

ers, the rose bushes that got a bit out of hand, and the enormous bird-of-paradise. "We had grown quite spoiled in that respect, but I did not have the faintest idea how I could translate such luxury to our loft here, where we had to make do without a garden." However, they did not take into account Harry Mayesh, the owner of a local flower store. "It was Harry who helped me realise what could be possible with only a few words," Puno recollects with a smile. "Try and experiment," he had said. "And if a plant dies, replace it with a new one." The concept was as simple as it was effective, because the collection keeps growing bigger and is in excellent condition. The big windows might play a major role as well, but Daniel also meticulously follows a neatly organised plant-care ritual every Friday.

GARDEN HOUSE

TOKYO JP

A green oasis in a densely populated district in Tokyo. Home and workplace to two authors and designed by Japanese architect Ryue Nishizawa, the Garden House is made of glass and harbours a miniature urban garden on every floor.

In bustling downtown Tokyo, nestled between two imposing office buildings, this extraordinary home is barely four metres wide, but attracts a great deal of attention. It is sometimes locally referred to as the vertical garden. The end result was a glass construction consisting of four 'floating' storeys, with no exterior walls or inner partitions.

The many plants and trees on every floor provide an adequate degree of privacy, but also allow maximum daylight access. Above all, it creates that unique sense of living outdoors for the building's owners, two authors who live and work here. It offers the opportunity to appreciate the lush greenery from every room.

The storeys are linked by a lightweight metal staircase that extends all the way to the top floor, through round openings in the floor plates. These openings also allow larger plants to keep growing all the way up to the roof terrace. It is striking to see indoor and outdoor plants co-existing side by side. The climate makes it possible, adding an extra dimension.

ATELIER ARTISTIQUE

MADRID ES

Nuria is happy for us to describe her home – a former dairy – as a cabinet of curiosities. In the early 1920s, fresh milk was sold here and there was a meadow, which is now a small garden. She moved in three years ago. As the owner of a vintage shop it was natural for her to surround herself with objects that have soul. She also loves art and plants, together with a good sprinkling of humour.

Nuria worked as a lifestyle journalist for *Spanish Vogue* for eight years. She recently started her own business, a vintage shop mainly selling items from the nineteen twenties, fifties and seventies. No wonder she has an eye for style and detail, and has managed to translate this idiosyncratically to her home around the corner from Retiro Park in the centre of Madrid.

"The opportunity to combine a green environment with the ever-vibrant life in the city persuaded me," says Nuria. "My grandma lived in a cottage – her garden was a jungle," she recalls. "She taught me to really appreciate nature. And she showed me that plants are good for you." Nuria is very keen to impart those values to her newborn twins. "Taking them for a daily walk in the park seems like an excellent start," she says with a smile.

Greenery plays an important role in her interior, too, and thanks to the immensely tall windows that look out on the garden she enjoys an 'outdoor feel'. The garden may be small, but it's exceptionally charming and optimally utilised. "I'd like it to be a bit more extravagant,' says Nuria, 'but it's a question of time and patience. The plants enjoy relatively good conditions here and can grow to cover up the stark concrete."

Inside the home the plants are clustered together in distinct groups. Nuria likes to sort and group the plants by size. And she's exceptionally good at combining particular types of plants with decorative items. She uses the greenery to bring balance and harmony to this eclectic interior.

Her secret when it comes to caring for plants? "I insist on using natural fertilisers, such as eggshells, banana tea and ash," Nuria reveals.

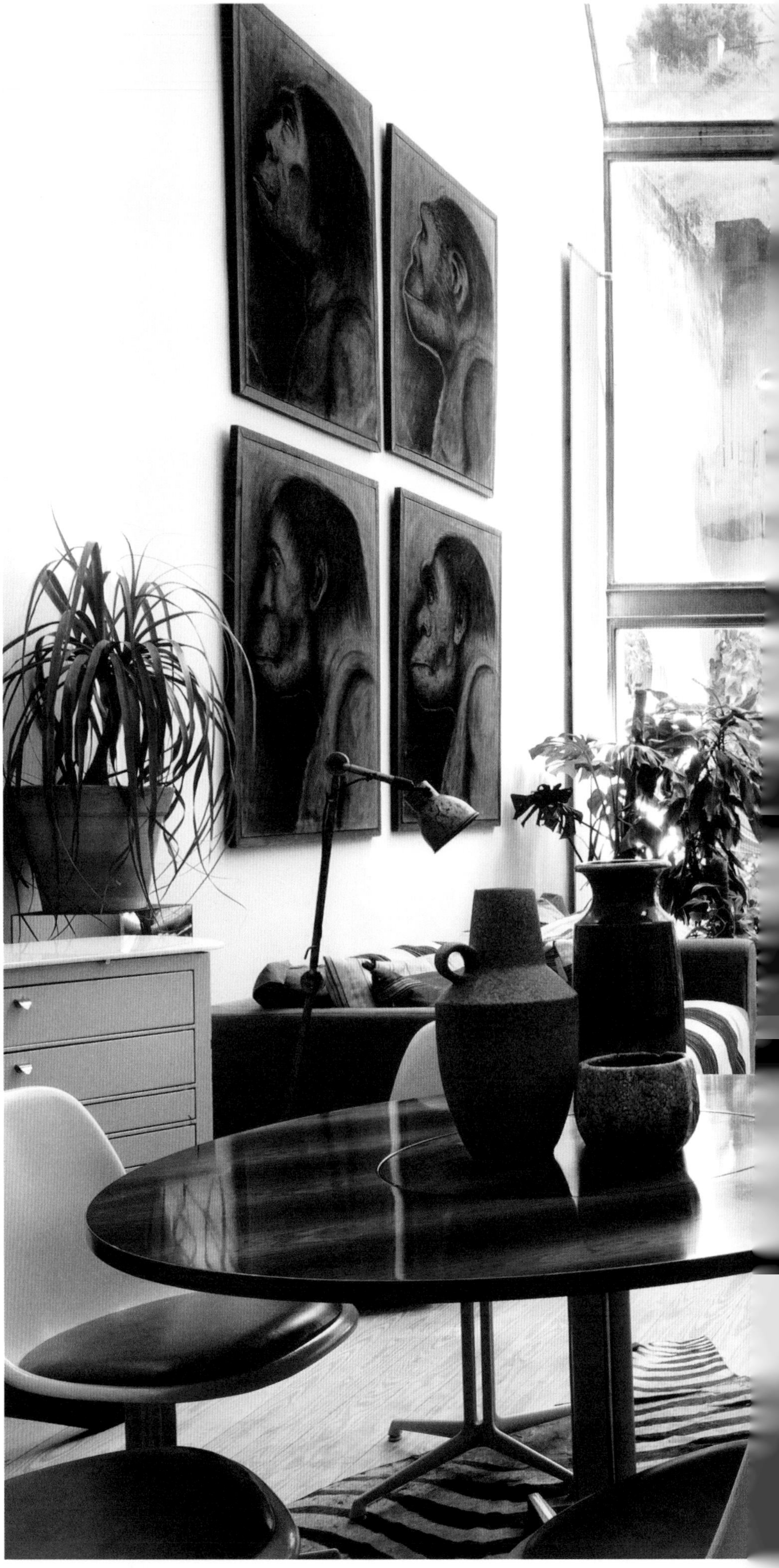

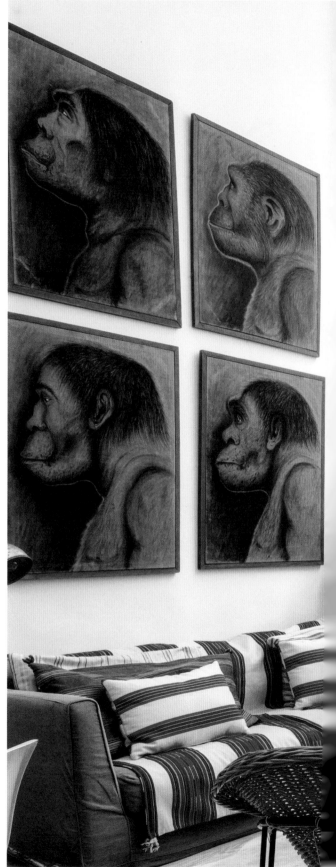

EXOTIC
EYE CATCHERS

BOSTON US

What happens when a project developer and interior designer work together to do what they love most: renovate houses? They put their heart and soul into it, and not just for a living wage. Serret and Miranda's home in downtown Boston has become the refuge they always dreamed of, an oasis in the heart of the always-busy metropolis.

Contractor and project developer Serret Ulises was the one who initially bought and renovated this property in downtown Boston: a coach house and manor house in Grand Victorian style. Later on, interior designer Miranda Melissa moved in with him and was eager to add her own personal touch. The place was renovated all over again. In addition to the kitchen, which was completely levelled and rebuilt, an extraordinary amount of attention was spent on the orangery, which is now their favourite place in the home.

The year that the couple spent in Barcelona inspired their desire for a Mediterranean lifestyle. The Moorish cement tiles and various souvenirs contribute to the overall impression, but the real eye-catchers are the plants, which are present in great numbers and huge sizes. It all started for Miranda when she bought a Philodendron at the age of 17, kicking off the start of a lifetime passion for plants. The orangery showcases several of her favourite species: the gaudy bird-of-paradise, the Mandevilla with its exotic, trumpet-shaped blossoms and a Philodendron from sheer nostalgia.

PRET-À-PORTER

PHILADELPHIA US

A former textiles factory in Northern Liberties, an artistic neighbour-hood in Philadelphia, is the home and workplace to stylist Elizabeth Sparacio and artist Jennifer Baker. Their shared love and passion for a green interior is the foundation for the warm and gentle ambiance of their home. The abundance of natural daylight is as striking as the charm of the well-preserved industrial character of the loft is endearing.

Once an industrial zone, today Northern Liberties is a flourishing district with boutiques and art galleries. Jennifer, who is a painter and sculptor, has been living in the house since 1978 and is very fond of the neighbourhood. "I have documented this district in my paintings over the course of years," she says. In the past thirty years, she has seen the neighbourhood evolve from a district with small rowhouses, factories and various breweries into an area featuring expensive houses and lofts. The sky-rocketing prices have ousted many residents from their houses, and many of the industrial buildings have been torn down. The building, which she has been sharing with Liz for the past few years, an old textile factory built in 1890, is one of the few buildings that remained standing.

Liz is very grateful to Jennifer for giving her the opportunity to move into this unique living and working environment.

"I was pleasantly surprised when I saw that the loft had undergone hardly any renovations," she says. "The welcoming feeling I felt when I first entered the loft was priceless."

Since Liz moved in, the interior of the loft has evolved from purely functional to modern and slightly eclectic. As a curator of vintage design, she has a keen eye for unique pieces. "I find inspiration in my job on a daily basis," she says, "and the loft we live in gives me every opportunity to experiment with that."

What both residents have in common is their weakness for plants in the home. Jennifer is rather nostalgic about the topic. "Every plant I have brought with me was once a cutting from the plants of my childhood home. They almost feel like family," she says with a smile.

It all feels very natural to Liz, who grew up in a green environment. Living in the city made her long for more greenery in the house. This longing did turn into a tale of trial and error as she was not familiar with choosing the right plants and caring properly for them. "Slowly but surely, I learned to sense which plants do well in this loft, but above all which ones really don't," Liz says. "That proved to be successful. I started to get enthusiastic about it, and soon wanted to expand our collection." To Liz, the shape and texture of a plant's leaves really matter. "Plants have a visual impact on the room and soften the industrial look."

The green wilderness owes its continued existence to the proper care it receives from the residents, as well as their pragmatic approach. "Survival of the fittest," they reasoned. "The loft, which is hard to heat in winter, and can barely be kept cool in summer, is not the most obvious place to keep plants. It is up to us to observe which plants can handle those extremes. It has been quite the search, but the right specimens are gradually in their proper place, and that's wonderful and satisfying," they conclude.

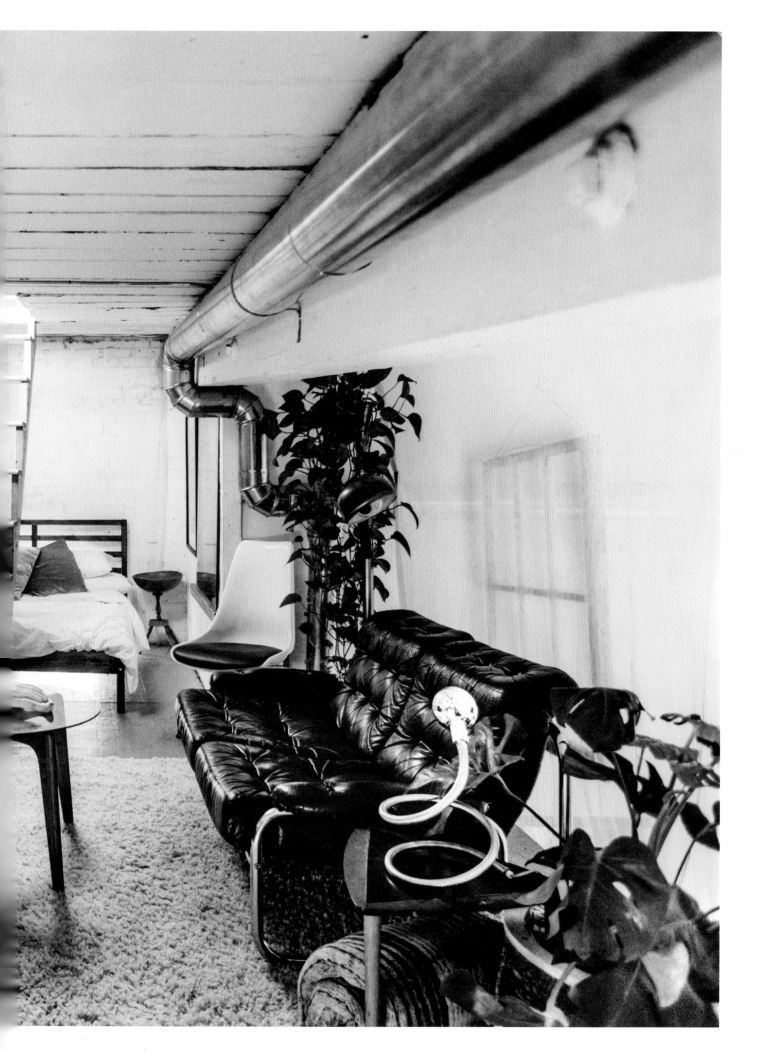

LOFT
CINEMATIC

MADRID ES

This industrial and colourful loft in downtown Madrid creates an almost cinematic backdrop. What takes the spotlight? The luscious and often exotic vegetation and the natural flood of daylight from above. It is unique because of the brutalist structures and distinctive materials. Actor and scriptwriter Gustavo Salmerón feels right at home here.

New York meets Berlin meets Brazil. That is exactly the eclectic mix that Gustavo had in mind while renovating his residence. The complete floor was stripped, and the rough structure of the concrete walls retained, providing the ultimate base for creating a home with an industrial character. The skylights in the roof, which provide a considerable amount of light, have been chosen deliberately.

By adding a substantial number of plants, especially the tropical varieties, Gustavo truly brings Brazil inside the house. Nature has found a perfect home here, enhancing the colourful aspect of the residence.

The plants are highlighted in wooden planters with metal handles that Gustavo found at antique shops. He put them on wheels so he could move the plants around, an efficient way to discover which plant does best in which location.

Moreover, it allows for a complete rearrangement of the layout of the loft every so often. The occupant wanted a residence with an organic interior, customisable to suit his moods. However, it is not just the plants that are mobile. The furniture, the kitchen cabinets, and even parts of the stairs: everything can instantly take on a different purpose. "I like the feeling of living somewhere else occasionally," Gustavo says with a smile.

There is no doubt that this is the home of a man with imagination. Gustavo loves giving second-hand furniture a new lease on life and reusing discarded materials. The kitchen has been built almost completely from recycled materials.

Gustavo has loved plants all his life. "As a child, my mother gave me the chore of watering the plants at appropriate times," he remembers vividly. "I took that duty very seriously. These days it has a therapeutic effect on me; it calms my mind." In his spare time, Gustavo loves to hang around in botanical gardens and greenhouses. "That hobby and a lifetime of consulting experts has taught me a lot about the particulars of plants," he tells us. "For instance, I know now that tropical plants require a lot of attention. It is important to keep a close eye on the humidity in your house and ventilate regularly, without allowing too much cold air in." But, Gustavo considers his plants worth the attention. "I would even say that your quality of life improves considerably when you surround yourself with plants."

URBAN GREEN

NEW YORK US

This elegant, spacious home is in Bedford-Stuyvesant, an upscale neighbourhood in Brooklyn, New York. Owner Greg Hahn collaborated with architect Eli Fernald on the renovations. Irene Park, the lady of the house, added her own green touches. Stylish, carefully chosen plants were situated in perfect places: a bright green accent here, a beautiful group of plants there.

Greg and Irene's house is bathed in daylight, allowing a diverse array of plants to flourish indoors. It's a great place for it too, as Irene believes that every room deserves its own botanic theme. In the bathroom, the custom-designed wooden rack might have been made especially to showcase green highlights. The Epipremnum and porcelain flower are in their element here; they thrive in humidity and are easy to cultivate in larger sizes.

The living room houses a nicely grouped collection of plants, varied in height and colour, with the vintage plant stands enhancing the overall impression. The leaf of the Philodendron in a planter on the mantelpiece adds a fresh note to the interior, while the palm tree achieves balance by providing bulk.

In the dining room, the greenery softens the industrial look of the space, while Irene took a more classical approach in the kitchen by putting smaller plants in terracotta pots. Irene particularly loves the warmth that the plants bring into the home. The fact that they purify the air was the deal breaker that inspired her to create a true indoor jungle.

INDOOR JUNGLE

LIER BE

"People sometimes tell me it's like I'm living in a forest. And I think it's fantastic!" exclaims Raf Verwimp. In Lier, a historic town near Antwerp, the flower-binder found his dream house in an old school building from the 1930s. His florist shop and decoration business are also located in this extraordinary building.

The store area is a perfect place for him to go wild with his decorations. It's unsurprising that he has plants in his home as well, and preferably the bigger types. The living room is situated in a former classroom with a soaring ceiling, as in its original state. Tall trees and giant plants fill the room, like the large mimosa, Heteropanax, Swiss cheese plant and Epipremnum. "It's almost like a dream come true to live here," Raf grins. "I was and still am in love with this house."

Raf takes care of the plants himself, which is a fairly easy task. "Although you do sometimes have to accept the odd falling leaf," he laughs. He doesn't have a favourite plant, but he does prefer plants that are easy to take care of. He enjoys seeing them grow. So where does his passion for big plants come from? "It makes me feel like the boundaries between outside and inside are blurring. It gives me a sense of security. And it's wonderful to read a book in a rattan chair, sitting under a tree by the window indoors."

MICRO AMAZONICA

MARINGA BR

The architects eagerly make use of the unique location of this concrete house, located at one of the highest points in the Brazilian city of Maringa. Its open floors and transparent windows provide Jeferson Hernades and his wife and children with very impressive views of the city and a permanent perspective on the luscious back garden.

He is an architect, she is a psychologist, and together they just love nature. Jeferson and Flavia shared a dream of designing a harmonious and functional house, overlooking the city and with a botanical back garden. By building that house at one of the highest locations in Maringa, they had already seen the first part come true. Une Arquitetura, a local architecture firm, designed a house with two floors, a roof terrace, large open rooms and transparent walls. The layout would allow the occupants to enjoy the city views to the fullest. Not to mention the back garden, an urban jungle of the exotic type, due to the prolific concrete and imposing green, which almost seems fused with it. There are plants in open soil, the Swiss cheese plant is majestic, and the occupants have chosen various types of hanging plants in concrete planters and climbing plants against the surrounding walls.

The structure of the residence is a textbook example of how the outdoors and indoors can be connected to each other. The luscious, garden vegetation has a huge impact on the interior. The residence almost seems to have been built around it. From the back garden, you can access the various floors of the residence – including the rooftop terrace, where vegetables and herbs are grown. They are used in the open kitchen in the back garden, which is used often and enthusiastically for cooking. "We love inviting friends and family over," says Jeferson. "That is why the garden so important to us. We find peace there, and if we can enjoy it in company, all the better."

Light and air are the key words within the house. The big bay windows provide daylight access and the lovely outdoor feeling. The rotating steel doors, which open onto the garage, ensure ample, natural ventilation in the house. And, the transparent garage doors also provide a connection with the street life.

The interior has a modern look and is functional. The wooden floors contrast nicely with the grey, stone ceilings and walls. Additionally, the finely detailed steel sculptures in front of the windows on the first floor soften the look of the concrete building.

Although there is not an abundance of plants indoors, the strategically placed hanging plants do enhance the feeling of spaciousness.

VERDANT CHARM

BENTVELD NL

Ten years ago, Anouk and her husband left their imposing house in the city for this home in Bentveld by the sea, which had everything they dreamed of: space, light and a view of the dunes. The sea of green in their home is everywhere, providing an intrinsic element in the ever-changing interior.

The Dutch photographer just happened to stumble across this house in Bentveld; it was love at first sight. When it was put up for sale a few years later, she had no trouble at all convincing her husband to move from the city to this gorgeous nature reserve. "A dream come true," she says.

The interior had been through many makeovers, depending on the latest trends. Anouk loves change and is constantly searching for fresh inspiration. The basis is light and fairly neutral, which makes variation mere child's play. "The palette of colours here was deliberately kept very basic," Anouk continues. "The colour in the home comes from the many plants we have, in all sorts of sizes and species."

Her love for nature has always been there, but the incorporation of greenery in the house was a gradual process. Thanks to her job as an interior photographer, plants regularly ended up in her home after a shoot. She frequently swaps plants with photographers and stylists in her network of friends. The huge variation in plants ensures that every room has its own atmosphere. There is the exotic palm in the living room, a lovely collection of hanging plants in the TV lounge, and the succulent in the hall with its bright, colourful blossoms. Various plants are grouped here and there in small clusters. A powerful example is the topsy-turvy table top in the spacious bedroom, which supports the perky flowering cacti beside the hanging begonia.

Taking care of the plants is sheer bliss for Anouk, done entirely on gut instinct. Her all-time favourite plant is the fern. "It's partly nostalgia, but it's mainly the elegant curl of the leaf before it unfurls that grabs my attention. A beautiful show put on by nature," she describes.

JUNGLE
OF LOVE

BALTIMORE US

In the greener part of the city of Baltimore, near the Hampden district along the banks of the Jones Falls River, an old cotton factory from 1870 was transformed into a luxury apartment complex. Today, it is more commonly known as Cotton Mill N°1. Hilton Carter, filmmaker, producer, and an interior decorator and plant specialist in his own right, found his dream loft there.

When I look out my bay windows, I can see the water of the river and the trees in the park," Hilton says. "You feel almost as if you are in the countryside, when you are actually living right in the heart of the city. That makes this place a unique location."

The historic building has been renovated with a flair for style. Original elements such as the concrete columns and the wooden floors were carefully preserved and contribute to the charm of this residential complex. As he had the option, Hilton did not hesitate, opting for a corner apartment in the building. It offers the perfect vantage point for his substantial collection of plants. "The amazing flood of light that enters the apartment gives me the option to provide room for a wide variety of plants, each with their own needs," says Hilton. It's impossible to miss: the lord of the manor loves, to put it mildly, a spot of greenery in his immediate living space. Moreover, it makes this residence what it truly is: a warm, pleasant place, where the owner's personality dominates the interior.

Even more than just a passion for plant life, Hilton cares deeply about diversity and combining various specimens.

Though it may look like a jungle, he did not place any of these plants at random. "I see a plant in the house as a design element," Hilton continues, "and especially with bigger specimens, you can set the tone and make a room even more warm and inviting. But place a *Ficus lyrata* (fiddle-leaf fig) between a *Monstera deliciosa* (swiss cheese plant) and a *Strelitzia* (bird-of-paradise), for instance, and you can see something almost magical happen. That process of discovering and unravelling is something that I thoroughly enjoy spending time on."

And, to be sure, spending time successfully, as it resulted in beautiful arrangements throughout the apartment. The test-tubes wall is just one of the many eye-catchers. That's precisely where all the new plants come to life: a solution for cutting plants that is as original as it is decorative. It's another one of Hilton's hobbies that has widely spread its roots.

If you ask him about his favourite, there is no hesitation in his answer. "The fiddle-leaf fig was my first big acquisition; she's been going strong for more than four years now. Together, we have navigated through lots of adventures," he says with a fond smile. "My biggest concern is keeping her in tip-top condition."

That the Carter home abides by a tight schedule to care for the nearly 150 plants – yes, they have indeed been counted – should not come as a surprise. "A basic knowledge of the different plants is vital," Hilton says. "Each plant comes with its own needs and its own specific treatment. I set my alarm so I know precisely when to water which plants." And then it is just a matter of following your gut instincts. You can get quite far with tender loving care. Rest assured, even I lose the occasional soldier," he jokes. It happens to the best of us.

DEPOT
BOTANIQUE

ANTWERP BE

In a depot building of a former distillery situated in Antwerp's
South (Het Zuid) district, Laurence Kluft has created a remarkable
loft following an ingenious renovation. The existing structure and
industrial character of the building were preserved. The interior
is a playful take on contrasts, intensely tangible in the successful
combination of plants and concrete.

All my life, I have been passionate about beauty, in all
of its forms," says interior
designer Laurence Kluft,
who started her career as
a fashion designer. She drew the design for
the renovation of her residence herself. She
was inspired by the Soviet architecture of
the 1970s – in the days when concrete was
combined with aluminium – and combined
it with her fondness for Japanese interiors.
"Even so, I often still hear that it almost
looks like a Brazilian city apartment," says
Laurence. That comparison makes sense, as
the apartment contains references to the
sleek architecture of Brazilian architect Pau-
lo Mendes da Rocha, with a botanical touch
of lush plants. Laurence elaborates, "My loft
ended up using softer tones. Even though the
concrete is visible, it is smoother and refined
in texture. For the walls, I spent a long time
searching for that perfect pigment to infuse
the 'cold' concrete with a 'warm' colour; I ended up choosing the colour of a sandy beach."

Beyond that vision for the loft, Laurence wanted to adopt a new perspective for the spaciousness of the building with her design and allow for a maximum amount of daylight access by excising internal volumes and installing large expanses of glass. On the first floor, now rebuilt into a yoga room, you can still see the original industrial details, the steel columns of the old storage space. The second floor, where she lives, rests upon a grid of 3 x 5 metres made from old, steel columns that were in poor condition. "We were unable to change anything about that grid, sadly," says Laurence, "and all the walls could only be built on that grid. That limitation spontaneously resulted in a new floor plan for the space, and the perfectly square form of the loft additionally brought out a natural *feng shui*. It was a challenge to create a functional and open living space with that limitation. Especially because my 'demands' were so wide-ranging: an entrance, large living room, desk, fireplace, media corner, eating area and kitchen."

The luscious plants help contribute to a Brazilian feeling in the house. The patio, which blurs the line between the outside world and the apartment's interior, received a concrete bench and a large planter containing an urban jungle that included bamboo, Gunnera, *Muehlenbeckia*, tree ferns and Italian cypress. The pond was placed with due respect for the *feng shui* of the house.

Inside, spread across the entire loft, the plants provide personal accents. Not an eclectic mix, but the right plant in the right place, providing the appropriate atmosphere for each room and every corner of the house – the striking African linden in the living area, the Swiss cheese plant with its beautiful dark leaves in the kitchen and the asparagus fern, thirsting for moisture, in the bathroom.

The carefully chosen green plants come perfectly into their own alongside to the sparse use of colour in the residence, the selection of vintage furniture, and distinctive decorations.

WUNDERKAMMER

AMSTERDAM NL

Master florists Florian Seyd and Ueli Signer have both been fascinated by nature since childhood. Operating under the name The Wunderkammer, the German term for cabinet of curiosities, they have been collaborating as floral artists and stylists for many years. Their house in Amsterdam is a spectacular reflection of their collaborative efforts. They have taken a very liberal interpretation of bringing nature into their home.

As a small boy, I was fascinated by caterpillars and frogs," says Florian, who moved to this Dutch metropolis from Germany. "But that love of animals gradually gave way to a passion for plants. I'm fascinated by botany." Ueli, who grew up in Switzerland, has always loved flowers and plants. Not only is he a florist and gardener, he designs furniture and aviaries as well. "If you take a close look at how plants and flowers are structured, you truly start to appreciate how wonderful and beautiful nature is," he says.

The house they live in, which is a cabinet of curiosities in its own right, is like wandering through the great outdoors. There's the butterfly collection that Florian inherited from his grandfather, the mounted giraffe head on the landing, the homemade penguin table in the bathroom, assorted antlers on the wall, and their own floral creations in gorgeous colours as a recurring theme throughout the house.

Florian's favourite plant in their home is the Musaceae, while Ueli favours the Myrtus. "No matter how beautiful an interior is, flowers and plant bring life into a home. And positive energy," they both agree. "Nature makes an interior more exciting and adds the finishing touches." Objects made from materials that originate from nature, like ceramics, glass, stone and wood, also add natural beauty and deserve their place in the home. "As long as it's made with love," Florian states firmly.

INTERIORS NOW! 2   TASCHEN

HUE   KELLY WEARSTLER

KELLY WEARSTLER ☉ DOMICILIUM DECORATUS

The Selby Is in Your Place

Mark Laita   Schlangen Serpentine

DIE GEHEIMEN GÄRTEN VON AMSTERDAM

MENZHAUSEN · DAS GRÜNE GEWÖLBE

LE JARDIN DE BOMARZO

MORE IS MORE

PLANTS AND
THEIR CARE

Plants are more or less permanent fixtures within our interior. Nearly everyone has a plant or something green that grows at home. Having plants makes us happy, and it is also very good for your health. Some just simply cannot get enough, and their collection of plants just keeps on growing, while others consider just a single plant at home to be the perfect amount of greenery.

Why do we do this, surround ourselves with greenery? We yearn for nature, for a place where we can find peace. We seek a place where we feel connected to what it is essentially all about: our origins. In previous times, we regularly went out and explored nature, yet nowadays we still yearn for our daily dose of green. Inspired by this desire, we are developing an increased appreciation of greenery in our immediate surroundings, in close proximity to the places we work or live.

Moreover, we seek this not only in spots where greenery is already abundant. We also use methods in cities to enjoy greenery more, both indoors and outdoors. We create vistas that cut straight through a house, looking out onto trees, plants and green rooftops. We install huge picture windows, turning nature into a framed painting and we build our living spaces around a patio, or an indoor garden, literally bringing nature inside the home. We surround our living spaces with plants that we place in such a way that they are clearly visible from various angles. Even given the limited space for greenery, this still makes it possible to create that feeling of being surrounded by greenery.

We are exploring the full potential and diversity of greenery. That could include large houseplants and trees. Or, it may mean even an entire wall covered with plants—another grand gesture in which minimal space is used for a maximum green effect. The plant is something that truly deserves to be seen. Accordingly, we spend more time on gorgeous variations of existing or known types and common houseplants, and we are always looking for unique specimens and distinctive plants with character.

A mundane houseplant picked up from a garden centre or nursery has actually fallen out of favour. To be sure, plants are at their most beautiful when they have stayed with us for some time. That is when they develop character, once they have adjusted to their surroundings. It can be observed from the position of the leaves as well as the stem or stalk growing towards the light. Nothing is more beautiful than an elongated stem bending towards the light. That does not mean that you should not buy any plants at a garden centre, but rather that you should specifically select plants that are still developing. If you want a distinctive plant with its own shape, you need patience. I prefer to buy my plants from some of my favourite growers or the older garden centres, where plants sometimes spend extended periods of time in one spot before being sold. Furthermore, you should also scour the Internet for plants that are offered second-hand. Fortunately, we are seeing fully matured plants more and more often in plant stores.

One thing is certain, though. Plants bring life to the places where we live, work and play, so we consider them indispensable in our interiors.

WHICH PLANT SHALL YOU CHOOSE?

We can only gaze with envy at beautiful and contemporary interiors with mature collections of plants or with a delightful, big Swiss cheese plant (Monstera deliciosa), *a bird-of-paradise* (Strelitzia nicolai) *or a sentry plant* (Agave americana). *Such are genuine statements in your interior design that shall only grow more beautiful when they spend more time 'living' with you. Anybody would like that, but how do you go about getting it? What is the secret behind these domestic jungles? What type of plant is actually the best match for you and your interior? What care do different types of plants require, and where should you place them? Gaining a deeper understanding of your plant's needs shall help you make this endeavour a success.*

INTERIOR

Before you start buying plants, it is wise to consider the placement of your plants and where you have enough space to place them. Do not merely consider which place would look nice with some greenery, but also whether the conditions in that spot would truly be suitable for your plants. When looking, also consider the amount of daylight when deciding on a spot. Some types of plants actually thrive in a shady spot, but all plants need at least some amount of daylight.

Try to consider your plants' needs, and make sure you put them in the correct spot from the start. Most plants don't tolerate being moved around. You can often tell by the colour of the leaves if a plant lacks sunlight; it will turn darker green, or the brightly coloured patterns on the leaves will fade. You can also adjust your interior and move some furniture around in order to create the proper setting. Are you planning a relocation or renovation? Then, it might be prudent to allocate room for your plants in the floor plan from the outset. You may decide upon plants in beautiful alcoves in a long stretch of wall, or an entire vertical wall covered with plants. These are possible ways to make your greenery an integral part of your interior design.

STATEMENTS IN YOUR INTERIOR DESIGN

Alocasia (Alocasia Zebrina)

banana, or dwarf Cavendish banana (Musa acuminata of Musa cavendish)

variegated rubber tree, rubber plant or rubber fig (Ficus elastica 'Tineke')

dwarf date palm (Phoenix roebelenii)

air plant (Tillandsia)

Heteropanax (Heteropanax chinensis)

sentry plant (Agave americana)

devil's backbone (Kalanchoë daigremontiana)

Philodendron (Philodendron 'Xanadu')

fishtail palm or toddy palm (Caryota mitis)

100-year-old aloe or sentry plant (Agave americana)

cactus or spurge (Euphorbia pseudocactus)

Chinese money plant (Pilea peperomioides)

kentia palm or thatch palm (Howea forsteriana)

·TIME

When you've decided where your plants will look best within your interior, you shall have to consider how much time you want to devote to their care. Are you the nurturing type? Then you may decide to buy plants that will need some extra TLC. Are you capable of completely forgetting about your plants, or are you frequently travelling? Then you had better buy some resilient plants that don't mind getting watered infrequently or irregularly. Truth be told, you can always go wrong with a plant, because that's just nature at work. However, if you take an honest look at yourself and your habits, you are sure to make this work.Start out with just a couple of plants and take it from there.

EASY· PLANTS

cactus

Epipremnum *or* Scindapsus (Epipremnum pinnatum or aureum, Scindapsus pictus)

Swiss cheese plant (Monstera deliciosa)

Chinese money plant (Pilea peperomioides)

spurge (Euphorbia pseudocactus)

mother-in-law's tongue or sanseveria (Sansevieria)

succulents, such as Crassula *and* Echeveria

fiddle-leaf fig (Ficus lyrata)

These plants are highly popular because they can thrive and survive in almost all conditions. A little too much shade or a day or two without water is no problem; these plants will be right as rain regardless. These plants are often also offered for sale on second-hand sites, as they do not need much care and can therefore grow quite old.

BUDGET

The budget you can afford is also a factor. Larger, more mature plants can be quite expensive, but there are younger plants available that are already quite big, and inexpensive. They grow even more beautiful over time. The same applies to plants that you buy smaller that will grow bigger very fast. You could consider swapping shoots or cuttings with your friends. Even if you are on a tight budget, you can still collect numerous attractive specimens.

FAST GROWERS

Epipremnum *or* Scindapsus (Epipremnum pinnatum or aureum, Scindapsus pictus)

velvet plant (Gynura aurantiaca)

Swiss cheese plant (Monstera deliciosa)

African linden (Sparrmannia africana)

Philodendron (Philodendron squamiferum and Philodendron selloum)

rubber tree, rubber plant, or rubber fig (Ficus elastica)

banyan fig (Ficus benghalensis)

asparagus fern (Asparagus plumosus or Asparagus setaceus)

chestnut vine (Tetrastigma voinierianum)

Japanese aralia or glossy-leaved paper plant (Fatsia japonica)

fiddle-leaf fig (Ficus lyrata)

spurge (Euphorbia pseudocactus)

HOW TO CARE FOR YOUR PLANT

Houseplants are usually indigenous species from somewhere else in the world that we took home with us, because we thought they were beautiful. Explorers used to do that to show them off and flaunt them in orangeries, and later on, they were cultivated domestically to put them in homes. This was our way of bringing nature into our homes and escaping the encroaching urbanisation. Plants from warmer continents are usually not suited to be kept outdoors in countries with another climate, because there it is either too cold or too wet. They stand a better chance of surviving in pots inside our homes. Some plants were able to survive in pots straight away, while others needed to be bred to thrive in a pot. These plants are still kept in our homes. It can be useful to know a bit more about the inner workings of plants and what they need. In short: plants need daylight and water. Nutrition and ambient temperature will also determine success. You shall need to find a balance amongst these factors for your plants.

ORIGINS

The best way to place plants is within an environment that matches the natural conditions of their original habitat. If you know the plant's origins, you can mimic its environment and provide the care it needs in order to help the plant grow and flourish as best as possible. If your plant originally came from dense, tropical forests, then it will thrive and look great in low-light, humid conditions. If you place this plant in direct sunlight, the plant's leaves will reflect this problem quickly. You don't have to recreate its habitat in every detail, but knowing its origins will help you better care for it. After a while, a plant will adapt to the conditions in your home and your care, and you will learn how to play around with the parameters. This will make the plants uniquely your own.

INDOOR PLANTS FOR OUTSIDE

banana, or dwarf Cavendish banana
(Musa acuminata or Musa cavendish)

dragon tree (Dracaena draco)

Swiss cheese plant (Monstera deliciosa)

Muehlenbeckia (Muehlenbeckia)

bird-of-paradise (Strelitzia)

soft tree fern
(Dicksonia antarctica)

succulents (for example, Kalanchoe or Echeveria, but place indoors in heavy rain)

Mexican fan palm (Washingtonia robusta)

Chinese windmill palm, or Chusan palm (Trachycarpus fortunei)

maidenhair (Muehlenbeckia)

paper plant or Japanese aralia plant
(Fatsia japonica)

LIGHT

Daylight matters tremendously to plants. If they don't get enough daylight, it limits the biological assimilation of the plant's leaves, so your plant will grow slowly, or not at all. Too much daylight will damage the leaves of some plants (scorching), arresting the assimilation process and resulting in all sorts of consequences. That means it is best to choose a spot for your plants that resembles its indigenous conditions as closely as possible. The amount of daylight your plant requires depends on its genus and where you place your plant. Some plants really thrive in plentiful, direct sunlight, while others do just as well in more shady conditions. Plants have certain characteristics from which you can deduce how much light they need, namely:

- Plants with tough, leathery leaves and thick stems, such as cacti and succulents or small-leaved plants, lose less water through evaporation, making them less prone to dehydration. That is why it is smart to place these plants near a window with southern exposure.
- Large-leaved plants or plants with delicate, branched leaves with a large surface area, such as swamp ferns or asparagus ferns (*Asparagus setaceus of plumosus*), shouldn't be placed in areas with too much sun. Ideally, you should place these plants farther from the window or near a window that has no direct sunlight, such as a window with northern exposure. The rubber plant (*Ficus elastica*), for example, does really well in low-light conditions.

HOW CAN YOU TELL IF YOUR PLANT IS GETTING TOO MUCH OR INSUFFICIENT DAYLIGHT?

If your plant is not getting enough daylight, you'll soon be able to tell by its growth pattern, that is, the stems will start to elongate. In other words, the plant's stems will grow longer and the spaces between the leaves will increase. Or you can tell by the size of the leaf, which will grow less big in a low-light environment. Sometimes you can tell by the colour of the leaves—they will turn darker green and the brightly coloured patterns on the leaves will fade.

TIP

You will soon become acquainted with your plant's requirements in different conditions by studying its colour and the soil in its pot. In low-light conditions, you may also want to decrease the amount of water. In brighter conditions, give your plant more water to prevent dehydration. In the end, it is all about balance. A good rule of thumb is that while all plants love daylight, not many can handle direct sunshine.

TIP

In order to catch as much sunlight as possible, all plants will turn their leaves and even their stems toward the light. Many plants that have been in your home for a while will take on a unique shape and form. If you desire a symmetrical, straight plant, you may want to turn it gradually on its axis rather than abruptly turning it a full 180°. The turning of the leaves is a slow process, and sudden changes will cause your plant to suffer from light deficiency.

PLANTS THAT DO NOT NEED MUCH DAYLIGHT

Aglaonema

Bromelia

Epipremnum *or* Scindapsus
(Epipremnum pinnatum or aureum, Scindapsus pictus)

Swiss cheese plant (Monstera deliciosa)

maidenhair fern (Adiantum hispidulum and Nephrolepis exaltata)

Chinese money plant (Pilea peperomioides)

Philodendron

rubber tree, rubber plant or rubber fig
(Ficus elastica)

Schefflera (Schefflera arboricola)

delta maidenhair fern (Adiantum raddianum)

fiddle-leaf fig (Ficus lyrata)

blue star fern (Phlebodium aureum)

Chinese evergreen (Aglaonema)

dwarf umbrella tree (Scheffera arboricola)

WATER

Plants need water. Watering keeps them fresh and firm. Additionally, water is needed to transport nutrients from the soil into the plant. These nutrients are converted into building blocks that will make plants grow and flourish.

WHAT KIND OF WATER SHOULD YOU GIVE YOUR PLANTS?

Ideally, you will give your plants natural rainwater. This is purer than tap water and contains almost no calcium, thus improving the solubility of soil nutrients. Due to the water purification process, tap water also contains other substances, such as various salts, which can be harmful to plants. Regardless of whether you give rainwater or tap water, always allow the water to reach room temperature before watering your plant. Otherwise the water will be too cold.

HOW OFTEN SHOULD YOU WATER YOUR PLANTS, AND HOW MUCH WATER SHOULD YOU GIVE THEM?

Water your plants judiciously. If you provide too little, your plants will get dehydrated. Or, if you give too much, the soil will stay too moist, allowing fungi and diseases a chance to affect the roots and capillaries and causing them to be unable to absorb water. If you water too much over a longer period of time, the soil will absorb so much water that there will be no oxygen left and your plant will effectively drown. Just like with providing the right amount of light, watering your plants boils down to close observation and sensing your plants' needs.

The amount and frequency of irrigation depends on the type of plant. Some plants, like succulents that store water in their stems and leaves, require less water than plants with big soft leaves, such as for instance an African linden *(Sparrmannia africana)*. Based upon these properties, you can divide plants into these three separate groups:
- Plants that need their soil to dry out between watering;
- Plants that sometimes need a little dry spell;
- Plants that need moist to wet soil.

At the end of this book, you can find an overview with watering guidelines for all the types of plants. The amount of water you give your plants each time

depends upon the climate where you live, the place in the room, the size of your plant and the size of the pot. In other words, two identical plants may have different watering needs depending upon their place in your home. For example, is the plant placed farther away from the window, thus receiving less daylight? If so, it will require less water, because the plant will evaporate less water. If you live in a warm climate or have very hot summers, you will need to increase the amount of water. Especially on hot days, an extra supply of water won't hurt, since plants need to evaporate water so they can cool down.

The size of the pot and the proportionate size of the plant are another factor. You'll need more water to moisten or soak the soil if your pot is larger. Larger plants naturally require more water than smaller plants, but you also need to make sure that you pour enough to properly soak the soil.

WATERING XXL PLANTS

Naturally, big plants in large pots require more water, and that is where things sometimes go wrong. Often these giants are overwatered or do not get enough water, and ultimately die. For the proper care of your XXL plant, it is therefore better to help the plant to absorb the water that it needs by opting for a semi-hydroculture solution. That process requires placing the plant in a closed pot in a watertight cover

on a layer of hydro grains or clay pellets, equipped with a water meter. The rest is filled up with potting soil. In the first weeks, you continue to pour water on the potting soil, and fill up the water meter a bit. In time, when the plant has grown water roots, you only water the plant by adding water to the water meter. The plant shall then absorb the water that it needs. If you do not want to set up a semi-hydroculture, use a pot with proper drainage and a saucer underneath.

HOW CAN YOU TELL IF YOUR PLANT IS GETTING TOO MUCH OR TOO LITTLE WATER?

You can determine how much water your plant needs by placing the pot on a dish and watering your plant until a layer of water forms in the dish. The amount of water retained in the pot is the amount you can safely pour every time you water your plants. If your plant receives too little water, it will dip into its reserves and wilt. Are the leaves hanging limp, and are they turning yellow and then brown? That is probably a sign your plant is getting too much water.

PLANTS THAT DO NOT NEED MUCH WATER

Bromelia (Bromelia)

cacti and succulents

air plant (Tillandsia, just mist or dip)

elephant's foot
(Beaucarnea recurvata or Nolina)

Yucca palm (Yucca elephantipes)

depressed clearweed and Chinese moneyplant
(Pilea depressa and Pilea peperomioides)

plants in a biosphere, terrarium in a bottle (once sealed, there is no longer any need for additional watering)

mother-in-law's tongue or Sanseveria
(Sansevieria)

Zanzibar gem (Zamioculcas zamiifolia)

AIR TEMPERATURE AND HUMIDITY

In addition to daylight and water, plants (and especially houseplants) require specific conditions in order to live and thrive. These conditions, such as humidity and temperature, differ everywhere. In a low-humidity climate or in an arid area, you will have to mist plants that prefer higher air humidity and/or place water containers near your heaters to increase your overall humidity. Even plants on a top shelf or in hanging baskets may need some additional fluids. Try to avoid major temperature differences between day and night and keep plants out of cold draughts. Do not place your plants near a large window on the sunny side of your home or near an outside door.

- Thick-leaved and thick-stemmed plants store water and will usually thrive in arid, warm conditions. They are also more tolerant of daylight as well as major temperature differences between day and night.
- Plants with feather-shaped leaves or big leaves thrive in an environment with higher humidity. You can mist them more often or place them in a humid bathroom for a day. It is best to mist your plant's leaves with rainwater as it is softer and doesn't leave calcium deposits on the leaves.

PLANTS MAKE YOU HAPPIER

Bringing greenery into your home increases your happiness, as research clearly shows. We've also finally figured out that plants are beneficial to people and their environment. Fresh air, as well as improved air quality, are important factors of this benefit. Our homes and buildings are insulated so well so as to save energy that they are often also completely closed off from fresh air, which we do need in order to function properly. We are aware that not everyone has a home with windows that can be opened wide, or a house that blends indoors and outdoors, creating a fresh flow of air and a healthy human environment. The air quality in your house or at work may well leave something to be desired, especially in the city. We know, smell and feel that plants can drastically improve the air quality in the house. Plants provide us with a dose of fresh air because they convert carbon dioxide (CO_2) into oxygen (O_2). In other words, the more plants you have in the house, the better it is. However, plants are capable of so much more. Plants also purify the air. The latest developments and studies show that plants can process certain air-borne substances. They are capable of absorbing volatile

organic compounds (voc) or chemicals from the air and converting them into nutrients. These potentially toxic substances enter our living environment through such channels as paint, flooring, detergents and insulation materials. Due to insufficient ventilation or air circulation in our homes and working environments, these substances remain in the air and can have an impact on our health. They may even accumulate to the point that we suffer from irritated eyes, headaches and concentration problems.

Aside from anything else, it would of course be prudent to start searching for materials that do not have such a major impact on air quality. We will also need to become more aware of the importance of nature in our environments, as plants can help us get rid of these volatile organic compounds or chemicals. For instance, architects could integrate plants into their projects so that greenery can become part of the actual architecture.

PURIFYING THE AIR

Because each plant is different and needs different nutrients, there are variations in plants absorbing different substances and in the extent to which plants absorb them. Some plants can absorb and convert significantly larger amounts of unhealthy substances, for instance. Chemicals such as formaldehyde, benzene, xylene, acetone, ammonia and various alcohols could be absorbed by the plant through its leaves. The beauty of it is that the plant continues to scrub those substances out of the air and never gets saturated. It continues to convert those substances into nutrients, storing them for its own use or converting them into energy. That energy is then used to make the plant grow and thrive. In addition to the leaves, the roots and micro-organisms in the soil surrounding the roots also absorb the substances; in essence, the entire plant purifies the air.

The glossary at the end shows the products that contain chemicals such as formaldehyde, benzene, xylene, acetone, ammonia and various alcohols.

BEST AIR PURIFIERS

sword fern (Nephrolepis exaltata)
→ filters the majority of formaldehydes and xylenes

dwarf date palm (Phoenix roebelenii)
→ very good filter for formaldehyde and xylene

bamboo palm (Chamaedorea seifrizii)
→ the very best filter for a considerable amount and variety of substances, such as formaldehyde, benzene, trichloroethylene and xylene

ivy (Hedera helix)
→ filters a reasonable amount of substances such as formaldehyde, benzene, trichloroethylene, xylene and ammonia, though also just a bit of everything

peace lily or white sails
(Spathiphyllum) → filters a considerable amount of formaldehyde, benzene, trichloroethylene, xylene and ammonia

dracaena (Dracaena deremensis)
→ is a very good filter for formaldehyde, benzene, trichloroethylene

mother-in-law's tongue or Sanseveria
(Sansevieria trifasciata) → filters formaldehyde, benzene, trichloroethylene and xylene

spider plant (Chlorophytum comosum)
→ filters formaldehyde and xylene reasonably well

banana (Musa Oriana)
→ filters formaldehyde

Epipremnum (Epipremnum aureum)
→ filters formaldehyde and benzene

Aloe (Aloe vera)
→ filters formaldehyde and benzene

rubber tree, rubber plant or rubber fig
(Ficus elastica) → filters formaldehyde

orchid (Dendrobium spp.)
→ filters ammonia

aglaonema

asparagus fern (Asparagus falcatus)

blue star fern (Phlebodium aureum)

Diefenbachia

peacock plant (Calathea makoyana)

Swiss cheese plant (Monstera deliciosa)

WHAT YOU CAN DO FOR YOUR PLANTS

We can also help plants purify the air by taking good care of them. In addition to watering them regularly – a sufficiently watered plant will thrive better and purify the air more effectively – you can help plants by reducing their stress as much as possible. External circumstances cause stress in plants, such as insects eating the leaves or sucking out their juices. Touch can also cause stress. Stress distracts plants, and will activate a variety of antibodies and defence mechanisms. That results in less energy spent on absorbing toxic substances from the air and purifying the air. It is best to leave the plant be so it can completely focus on its own internal processes and therefore on absorbing and processing substances. Limiting touch and rotating and moving plants as little as possible will help them stay relaxed.

NUTRITION

In general, when you first buy a plant, the potting soil that comes with it will contain sufficient nutrients for the first couple of months. The soil requires no extra attention from you. After a period of time, particularly in Spring during the growing season of most plants, you would do well to feed your plants a little extra. This feeding can be achieved by adding liquid plant fertilisers to the water you give them. It's best to use an organic fertiliser. Stick to the dosage mentioned on the bottle! Otherwise you might damage the roots. Another method for feeding is adding pellets or granulated fertilisers to the soil, which will release their nutrients slowly.

After a while, once the soil is truly exhausted, you should replace the soil by re-potting your plants. This is also an excellent opportunity to move your plant to a bigger pot. You'll need to remove the plant from the pot and carefully loosen the old potting soil from the root ball and between the longer roots. Put a layer of new potting soil in the bottom of the pot, place the root ball on top, and fill the pot up with additional soil. Tamp the loose soil down lightly and water your plant. You can give your plant an extra boost by soaking it in a bucket of water the day before, pot and all.

TIP

If you own large pots with plants that have a long, thick stem or trunk, you could decide to fill the edges of the pot with smaller plants or hanging plants.

SELECTING THE RIGHT POT FOR YOUR PLANT

The pot makes the plant, so choose it with care. For instance, select a colour and material that is balanced in interaction with your interior and where it will be placed. For example, a grey pot on a grey floor or a neutral-coloured pot on an unpainted wooden side table looks gorgeous. Or, you can achieve balance by using matching pots, such as choosing pots all made of the same material or all in the same colour. Sometimes it can be quite effective to go for bold contrasts, adding striking highlights in your home. It may pay off to experiment a little.

When shopping for a pot, decide on one that goes well with your plant. Don't choose a pot that is too small, because it will limit your plant's ability to grow; plants do not respond well to that limitation. Choose a pot that matches your plant's size to prevent it from constantly tipping over. Make sure that the size above ground is in balance with the size of the roots below the soil. There is a wide range of materials to choose from, not to mention pots with and without drainage holes. Decided on a pot with a drainage hole? Then you should put a saucer underneath to contain the excess water. If you've selected a pot without a drainage hole, you should put a layer of clay pellets on the bottom to make sure the roots are not constantly under water, where they might rot. If the opportunity arises and you have the room to grow gorgeous, larger plants, you could consider placing them in built-in planters or even directly into the soil. This will make your plants even more a part of your home.

THE PLANT DOCTOR

How do you deal with day-to-day problems?

1. **The bottom leaves turn yellow and fall off:**
    → Allow the soil to dry thoroughly, then give the plant less water from that point on.

2. **Leaves are hanging limp and drying out:**
    → Give the plant more water.

3. **Leaves are hanging limp and drying out, even though you water it sufficiently:**
    → Put the plant in a less draughty spot, or in a higher spot farther from the cold floor.

4. **Leaves are developing brown edges:**
    → Place the plant closer to the window or in a different spot that receives more light.

5. **Leaves have yellow or brown patches:**
    → Place your plants farther from the window or in a spot that's less sunny.

6. **Leaves suddenly fall off:**
    → Place the plant in a spot that has no draught or has a constant temperature.

7. **Brightly coloured leaves turn green and the pattern fades:**
    → Provide more daylight for the plant to restore the coloured pattern.

8. **Plant hardly grows, or does not grow at all:**
    → During growth period or in the Spring, provide more daylight for the plant or put the plant in a larger pot.

9. **The potting soil is turning white on top:**
    → Give rainwater and replace the top layer of soil.

10. **Leaves develop white patches:**
    → Check for insect infestation.

11. **Leaves curl up or develop holes:**
    → Check for insect infestation.

PLANTS IN
EACH INTERIOR

WABI-SABI

1   COMMON FIG
Ficus carica

2   ELEPHANT'S EAR
Alocasia calidora

3   CALATHEA
Calathea veitchiana

A more striking contrast cannot be imagined: the natural shapes and the fresh greens of the plants in terracotta pots against the grey concrete. In this apartment, they matter, all of these large plants of various heights. In a basement apartment such as this, the light from above ensures that the plants are able to grow properly. If you have less light, consider installing special lamps that encourage plant growth.

CINEMA FLORA

1 **SWISS CHEESE PLANT**
Monstera deliciosa

2 **UMBRELLA PLANT**
Cyperus alternifolius

3 **FIDDLE-LEAF FIG**
Ficus lyrata

4 **SPIDER PLANT**
Chlorophytum comosum

5 **GUIANA CHESTNUT, SABA NUT or MONEY TREE**
Pachira aquatica

6 **BIRD-OF-PARADISE**
Strelitzia reginae and nicolai

7 **MAIDENHAIR**
Muehlenbeckia

8 **EPIPREMNUM**
Epipremnum pinnatum or Scindapsus

The former cinema owned by Attilio Solzi and Paola Galli is a perfect environment for plants, due to the space and ample daylight. Indoor flora looks particularly lovely in elevated areas, like a mezzanine, giving plants room to grow both upwards and downwards. Plants that thrive in less sunny spots, like the Swiss cheese plant (*Monstera deliciosa*) and the fiddle-leaf fig (*Ficus lyrata*), should be set farthest from the window or behind other plants. These plants and the flowering *Epipremnum vines* (*Epipremnum pinnatum or Scindapsus*) can grow quite large, so it's best to give them lots of room. Many plants can handle lower-light environments, although they will grow more slowly, produce fewer leaves and develop longer stems. You can supplement high-profile greenery by adding smaller, fast-growing species like spider plants (*Chlorophytum comosum*).

GREEN, GREY & GLAMOUROUS

1 SWISS CHEESE PLANT
Monstera deliciosa

2 SPIDER ALOE
Aloe vera spinosissima

3 SUCCULENTS
Echeveria elegans

4 SENTRY PLANT
Agave americana

5 FRAGRANT DRACAENA
Dracaena fragrans

6 SNAKE PLANT or MOTHER-IN-LAW'S TONGUE
Sansevieria trifasciata

7 DESERT CABBAGE
Kalanchoe NF thyrsiflora

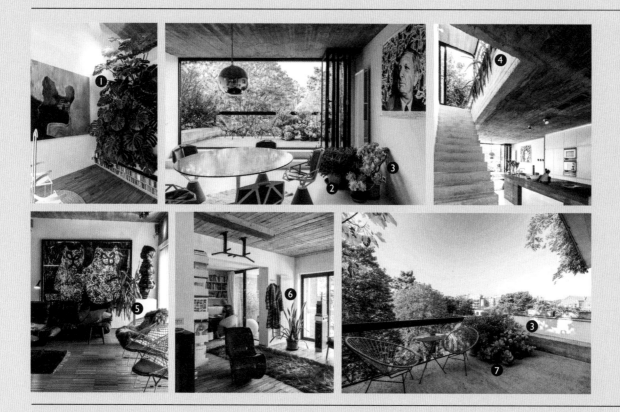

We adore those bold statements! One really big houseplant immediately achieves a major impact. This will not just create the feeling of a jungle of plants, but also the feeling that you can hide in it. That feeling alone is already a reason to invest in a seriously large plant. You can also start a little smaller and allow the plant to grow and expand by giving it space. A Swiss cheese plant (*Monstera deliciosa*) or another *Philodendron* would be very suitable for that, because they continue to grow. This interior in Antwerp truly brings out the beauty of these giants due to the contrast between the gorgeous, round shapes of the leaf and the roughness of the concrete. In addition, the singnificantly overgrown succulents also provide a wondrous statement. They can be left outdoors in summer months. However, if it rains hard for a long time, remember to move them to dry shelter, or else they will drown.

ASIAN DREAM

1 BANYAN FIG
Ficus benghalensis

2 COCONUT TREE
Cocos nucifera

3 PHILODENDRON
Philodendron 'Imperial Red'

4 ANTHURIUM or LACELEAF
Anthurium

5 FAN PALM or ROUND LEAF FAN PALM
Livistona rotundifolia

6 CALADIUM
Caladium

7 CHERRY LAUREL
Prunus laurocerasus

8 BOUGAINVILLE
Bougainvillea

9 PURPLE SHAMROCK
Oxalis triangularis

Tropical climates have the advantage in that many plants will already feel at home there because of the favourable temperature and humidity. That means that indoor and outdoor plants combine very well in big cities located in tropical countries, and this usually provides for gorgeous vegetation. The circumstances are ideal for these frequently indigenous plants. Plants that are for sale as houseplants in slightly cooler countries could basically just be retrieved straight out of the local plant life there. A nice example is the coconut tree (*Cocos nucifera*), which might struggle as a houseplant in cooler climates, particularly in winter months. Here in these tropical climates, they can just grow around the home, preferably in open soil.

PARIS TEXAS

1 DRAGON TREE
Dracaena marginata

2 JACARANDA TREE
or GREEN EBONY TREE
Jacaranda mimosifolia

3 MOTH ORCHID
Phalaenopsis

4 KANGAROO PAW
Anigozanthos

5 DEVIL'S BACKBONE
Kalanchoe daigremontiana

6 SPURGE
Euphorbia pseudocactus

7 PAPER PLANT
or JAPANESE ARALIA
Fatsia japonica

The house owned by Nathalie Wolberg and Tim Stokes is awash in daylight, with big windows that provide almost no boundaries between indoors and outdoors. This intensifies the sense of living in nature. Boundaries blur even more because the big dragon tree (*Dracaena marginata*) is planted in the soil indoors, while the flowering Jacaranda tree (*Jacaranda mimosifolia*) grows in pots both inside the house and outside in the garden. Many of the windows can open wide, bringing the outdoors inside. Plants love the fresh air, especially in summer!

OFICIO STUDIO

1 **DWARF UMBRELLA TREE**
Schefflera arboricola

2 **SUCCULENT**
Rhipsalis monacantha

3 **RUBBER FIG**
Ficus elastica

4 **STAGHORN FERN**
Platycerium bifurcatum

5 **ELEPHANT'S EAR**
Alocasia amazonica

6 **HONEYSUCKLE**
Lonicera periclymenum

7 **SPIDERWORT**
Tradescantia

8 **SPIDER PLANT**
Chlorophytum comosum

9 **ASPARAGUS FERN**
Asparagus setaceus or plumosus

10 **PORCELAIN FLOWER or WAX PLANT**
Hoya carnosa

11 **SWISS CHEESE PLANT**
Monstera deliciosa

12 **100-YEAR-OLD ALOE or SENTRY PLANT**
Agave americana

Melina and David's charming old building is where they live, work and grow an amazing array of plants. The climate allows house plants to thrive outdoors and outdoor plants like honeysuckle (*Lonicera periclymenum*) to do very well indoors. The plants are generally situated in light spots near a window or by the door to the roof terrace. Here they get indirect light – an ideal situation for the plants to grow.

GREEN DIY DREAM

1 **RUBBER PLANT OR RUBBER FIG**
Ficus elastica 'Tineke'

2 **DRAGON TREE**
Dracaena marginata

3 **PHILODENDRON**
Philodendron martianum

4 **OCTOPUS TREE**
Schefflera actinophylla 'Amante'

5 **FIDDLE LEAF FIG**
Ficus lyrata

6 **KENTIA PALM**
Howea forsteriana

7 **ORCHID**
Cymbidium

In a transparent house with lots of windows, one large plant is enough to give a green feel and keep the space open and airy. The space around the house also plays an important role in ensuring the presence of greenery. Where there is a lot of (indirect) light, you can really grow any plant successfully. Attractive plants with an open structure like the dragon plant or dragon blood tree (*Dracaena marginata*), the octopus tree (*Schefflera actinophylla* 'Amante') and the rubber plant or rubber fig (*Ficus elastica* 'Tineke'), which has already grown towards the light, will work very well here. To allow your plants to grow in their own way and give them space, shorten the supports by half once they're well established. You can remove them entirely after a while.

SCANDINAVIAN IMMACULACY

1 OLIVE TREE
Olea europaea

2 DWARF BANANA TREE
Musa acuminata

3 BLUE STAR FERN
Phlebodium aureum

4 ELEPHANT'S EAR
Kalanchoe beharensis

5 CHRISTMAS CACTUS
Schlumbergera or Epiphyllum

6 MINT GERANIUM
Pelargonium tomentosum

**7 HANGING ASPARAGUS
or ASPARAGUS FERN**
Asparagus densiflorus

8 BLUE CHALK FINGERS
Senecio mandraliscae

9 MIMOSA
Acacia dealbata 'gauloise'

Inspired by the gorgeous orangery in this blond wood interior, plants very naturally find their own way. White and wood combine beautifully with the grey-green leaves of the elephant's ear (Kalanchoe beharensis), blue star fern (*Phlebodium aureum*) and olive trees (*Olea europaea*). These plants were carefully selected for their gorgeous, subtly muted green shades. The bright green of the dwarf banana tree (*Musa acuminata*) and the small hanging pots with garden herbs offer a nice contrast and link indoors and out-doors. Displaying plants in lovely little clusters gives the house a beautiful botanic touch, which is underlined by the use of glassware, like the bell jars and the hanging garden herb holders.

FRENCH GRANDEUR

1 LEAF BEGONIA
Begonia mazae

2 DWARF UMBRELLA TREE
Schefflera arboricola

3 FICUS TREE OR WEEPING FIG
Ficus benjamina

4 MACHO FERN
Nephrolepis exaltata

5 DELTA MAIDENHAIR FERN
Adiantum venustum and Adiantum tenerum

6 PARLOUR PALM
Chamaedorea elegans

7 ANTHURIUM
Anthurium andraeanum

8 BAMBOO
Bambusa vulgaris

9 BABY'S TEARS
Soleirolia soleirolii

10 REX BEGONIA
Begonia rex

Simply spectacular: a complete jungle wall filled with plants that can grow freely and run as wild as they like. No tidy ferns placed neatly in a row, but a living tapestry focused on one, central place, making full use of the complete height. This wall full of plants achieves maximum impact as a result. By choosing plants that can still grow bigger and fuller, you can get closer to nature. Some plants thrive better than others and you can see how nature works. The occasional plant shall disappear, while another might acquire more territory. In addition to a gorgeous and aesthetic impression, the wall also contributes to a healthy indoor environment. Due to the air-purifying effect of plants – some in particular, such as the dwarf umbrella tree (*Schefflera arboricola*) and the macho fern (*Nephrolepis exaltata*) – this wall provides fresh air and is therefore good for your health.

GREEN STATEMENTS

1 100-YEAR-OLD ALOE
or SENTRY PLANT
Agave americana

2 PENCIL TREE
or FIRESTICK PLANT
Euphorbia tirucalli

3 DRAGON TREE
Dracaena draco

4 CHINESE MONEY TREE
Crassula ovata

5 CACTUS
Cactus cereus

Plants occupy a prominent position in this former factory in Milan. They have become major statements in the house, not just because of their size, but also due to the metal structures that artist Antonino Sciortino created to support the plants. In the stair-well, for instance, he made a metal rack on trolleys to hold the succulent cactuses (*Cactus cereus*). When you use huge plants, like this giant 100-year-old aloe (*Agave americana*), you don't need many to create an imposing impact in rooms of all sizes.

INDOOR PATIO

1 **KENTIA PALM or THATCH PALM**
Howea forsteriana

2 **BROMELIA or VRIESEA**
Vriesea seideliana

3 **PRAYER PLANT**
Maranta leuconeura

4 **PHILODENDRON**
Philodendron selloum

5 **ELEPHANT'S EAR**
Alocasia calidora

6 **ARECA PALM**
Chrysalidocarpus lutescens

7 **BIRD'S NEST FERN**
Asplenium nidus

8 **PHILODENDRON**
Philodendron martianum

9 **BROADLEAF LADY PALM or BAMBOO PALM**
Rhapis excelsa

10 **PEACE LILY**
Spathiphyllum

11 **ZANZIBAR GEM**
Zamioculcas zamiifolia

Direct from nature into your house. Conditions as close as possible to their natural habitat are where the South American *Philodendron* and zebra plant grow best. Just as in the rainforest, these indigenous plants feel most at home in the filtered light of the patio under the open, concrete grid and beneath the awning by the entrance. There they are protected from the harsh rays of the sun, but they do benefit from daylight, warmth and rainwater. 'Outside' is literally brought inside.

BOTANIC ELEGANCE

1 **FIDDLE-LEAF FIG**
Ficus lyrata

2 **DWARF UMBRELLA TREE**
Schefflera arboricola

3 **REX BEGONIA**
Begonia rex

4 **CALATHEA or PRAYER PLANT**
Maranta leuconeura

5 **UMBRELLA PLANT**
Cyperus alternifolius

6 **CROWN FERN**
Aglaomorpha coronans

7 **RABBIT'S FOOT FERN**
Humata tjermannii

The plants have been meticulously selected to finish off the interior. Green makes the interior. There are lovely statements like a sizable fiddle-leaf fig (*Ficus lyrata*), but also beautiful, subtle plants with a lovely leaf pattern, such as the rex begonias (*Begonia rex*). They go very nicely with the wood of the sideboard. By taking a good look at your interior, you can find inspiration for which plants to select. The bathroom boasts a well-chosen swamp plant that loves humidity: the umbrella plant (*Cyperus alternifolius*).

PASTEL PERFECT

1 **PARLOUR PALM**
   Chamaedorea elegans

2 **RUBBER PLANT**
   or RUBBER FIG
   Ficus elastica 'Tineke'

3 **SKELETON PLANT**
   or ALOCASIA
   Alocasia amazonica

4 **SNAKE PLANT**
   Sansevieria trifasciata

5 **SWISS CHEESE PLANT**
   Monstera deliciosa

6 **BROADLEAF LADY PALM**
   Rhapis excelsa

7 **FIDDLE-LEAF FIG**
   Ficus lyrata

8 **PHILODENDRON**
   Philodendron selloum

9 **DRAGON TREE**
   Dracaena marginata

10 **PHILODENDRON**
   Philodendron 'Imperial Red'

11 **ARECA PALM**
   Chrysalidocarpus lutescens

12 **PEACE LILY**
   Spathiphyllum

13 **ELEPHANT'S EAR**
   Alocasia calidora

14 **BIRD-OF-PARADISE**
   Strelizia nicolai

15 **ANTHURIUM**
   Anthurium

16 **PHILODENDRON**
   Philodendron scandens

17 **EPIPREMNUM**
   Epipremnum aureum

Plants placed in a room with perfectly filtered light, and which are also routinely cared for, are plants in top condition. And, it shows. The plants look fresh and full and the leaves show no dry, scorched edges or spots. In the summer months, these plants will thrive here, because it will be light for a longer period of time, just when the plants are entering their growing season. Exotics such as the bird-of-paradise (*Strelitzia nicolai*) will especially do very well here and can grow extremely large. Puno and Daniel had to grow used to the idea of no longer having a garden in their new house, but they have managed to bring the garden indoors in a very beautiful way. Grouping the plants makes it possible to create a grand effect – much grander than placing plants as separate, green islands. Especially on the giant red sofa, you truly experience the grouped greenery as a garden inside the house.

GARDEN HOUSE

1. **NEW ZEALAND FLAX**
   Phormium tenax

2. **MEXICAN DWARF PALM**
   Chamaedorea

3. **PHILODENDRON**
   Philodendron xanadu

4. **BIRD'S NEST FERN**
   Asplenium nidus

5. **DWARF UMBRELLA TREE**
   Schefflera arboricola

6. **JACARANDA TREE**
   or GREEN EBONY TREE
   Jacaranda mimosifolia

7. **CRINUM LILY or SPIDER LILY**
   Crinum asiaticum

8. **KANGAROO PAW**
   Anigozanthos

9. **LAVENDER**
   Lavandula angustifolia

Greenery plays a role on every floor, in a gorgeous combination of indoor and outdoor plants, transforming this house into a vertical forest: a green oasis in downtown Tokyo. It also houses flowering plants, like a jacaranda tree or a green ebony tree (*Jacaranda mimosifolia*), crinum lily or spider lily (*Crinum asiaticum*), kangaroo paw (*Anigozanthos*) and lavender (*Lavandula angustifolia*). The liberal use of glass, internal openings and doors that can open all the way optimise daylight access for the plants. The interior landscaping design has even taken into account the growth patterns of trees on the terrace by providing a large round hole on the top floor. If your rooftop plants are expected to grow tall, do keep in mind that flower pots and planters dry out faster when exposed to sun and wind. An irrigation system can help keep your terrace plants hydrated.

ATELIER ARTISTIQUE

1 ELEPHANT'S FOOT
Beaucarnea recurvata

2 MISTLETOE CACTUS
Rhipsalis cassutha

3 CHINESE MONEY TREE
Crassula ovata

4 ASPARAGUS FERN
Asparagus setaceus or plumosus

5 EPIPREMNUM
Epipremnum aureum

6 SWISS CHEESE PLANT
Monstera deliciosa

7 DRAGON TREE
Dracaena fragrans

8 MONEY TREE
Pachira aquatica

9 BIRD'S NEST FERN
Asplenium nidus

10 SPINELESS YUCCA
Yucca elephantipes

11 PEACE LILY
Spathiphyllum 'Sensation'

12 JAPANESE ARALIA
or GLOSSY-LEAVED PAPER PLANT
Fatsia japonica

The most beautiful thing about this studio house is the jumble of indoor and outdoor plants, all adapted to the location where they have been placed. Although this house has big windows, the sunlight does not enter directly due to the walls around the garden, which is just perfect for many types of plants. This is true not only with respect to light intensity, but also in terms of temperature fluctuations. For instance, this place shall never get extremely warm, nor cold. The patio is perfectly suited to place houseplants such as the glossy-leaved paper plant or Japanese aralia plant (*Fatsia japonica*), the spineless yucca or giant yucca (*Yucca elephantipes*) and the Swiss cheese plant (*Monstera deliciosa*) outside in the spring and summer months. The paper plant can remain outdoors throughout the year, even in cooler climates.

EXOTIC EYE CATCHERS

1 BIRD-OF-PARADISE
Strelitzia reginae and nicolai

2 MANDEVILLE
Mandevilla

3 SNAKE PLANT
or MOTHER-IN-LAW'S TONGUE
Sansevieria

4 SWISS CHEESE PLANT
Monstera deliciosa

5 ELEPHANT'S EAR
Alocasia amazonica

6 PHILODENDRON
Philodendron xanadu

7 FIDDLE-LEAF FIG
Ficus lyrata

8 DWARF BANANA TREE
Musa acuminata

9 EPIPREMNUM
Epipremnum pinnatum or Scindapsus

A house as spacious and light as this Boston residence is a perfect environment for lush, green plants to flourish. Ideally, they should be kept in large pots (appropriate to the size of the plant) to maintain a good plant-pot ratio and give the plants enough room to grow big and strong. The visible growth above the soil has its counterpart underground; healthy roots make for healthy plants. The bird-of-paradise (*Strelitzia reginae and nicolai*) and the *Epipremnum* (*Epipremnum pinnatum or Scindapsus*) do very well here. Moreover, larger pots can accommodate low-growing vegetation along the edges, supplementing the taller plant in the centre. Just one more reason to go for the really big planters!

PRÊT-À-PORTER

1 EPIPREMNUM
Epipremnum aureum

2 PHILODENDRON
Philodendron selloum

3 KENTIA PALM OR THATCH PALM
Howea forsteriana

4 ALOE
Aloe vera

5 AGLAONEMA
Aglaonema modestum

6 NORFOLK ISLAND PINE
Araucaria heterophylla

7 PHILODENDRON
Philodendron 'Xanadu'

8 BIRD-OF-PARADISE
Strelitzia nicolai

**9 SCHLUMBERGERA
or CHRISTMAS CACTUS**
Schlumbergera

10 ARROWHEAD PLANT
Syngonium podophyllum

11 TRIANGLE CACTUS
Acanthocereus tetragonus

12 PHILODENDRON
Philodendron scandens

13 SWISS CHEESE PLANT
Monstera deliciosa

In a spacious, open area, such as in this old textile factory, you can create gorgeous sheltered nooks using plants. All it takes is a few tall specimens and several smaller plants. This factory provides plenty of light for a wide variety of plants; as most of them shall thrive. Do note that the seasons can be quite a challenge in the larger, older and often less well-insulated rooms. In the summer months, when the temperature rises considerably, you will need to give the plants more water and more often. In winter months, when the rooms are hard to heat, they need considerably less water.

LOFT CINEMATIC

1 ELEPHANT'S EAR
Alocasia odora

2 BANANA
Musa acuminata 'Super Dwarf Cavendish'

3 FALSE SARSPARILLA
Hardenbergia violacea

4 CHILEAN HARD FERN
Blechnum chilense

5 umbrella bamboo
Fargesia murieliae

The bright green hues of the elephant's ear (*Alocasia odora*), the banana (*Musa acuminata 'Super Dwarf Cavendish'*) and the false sarsparilla (*Hardenbergia violacea*), combined with the mustard-coloured and orange-red elements, especially provide a colourful ambiance to this house. The false sarsparilla is the odd one out here as the bright-green colour that the plant has developed is due to a lack of light. By using sizeable planters–providing an effect that they were planted in open soil, but then indoors–they get plenty of space and can grow quite large.

URBAN GREEN

1 KENTIA PALM or THATCH PALM
Howea forsteriana

**2 SNAKE PLANT
or MOTHER-IN-LAW'S TONGUE**
Sansevieria

3 RUBBER FIG
Ficus elastica

4 PHILODENDRON
Philodendron xanadu

5 FIDDLE-LEAF FIG
Ficus lyrata

6 EPIPREMNUM
*Epipremnum pinnatum
or Scindapsus*

7 SPURGE
Euphorbia pseudocactus

**8 GUIANA CHESTNUT, SABA NUT
or MONEY TREE**
Pachira aquatica

9 PORCELAIN FLOWER or WAX PLANT
Hoya carnosa

The plants in this apartment lend a softer touch to the textured rawness of the unplastered walls, concrete and wood, bringing the home to life. The tall fiddle-leaf fig (*Ficus lyrata*) and the long tendrils of the *Epipremnum* (*Epipremnum pinnatum or Scindapsus*) are like veins running through the house, creating a pleasant atmosphere.

INDOOR JUNGLE

1 HETEROPANAX
Heteropanax chinensis

2 MIMOSA
Acacia dealbata 'gauloise'

3 SWISS CHEESE PLANT
Monstera deliciosa

4 EPIPREMNUM
Epipremnum pinnatum or Scindapsus

5 CHINESE MONEY TREE
Crassula ovata

The big trees like the *Heteropanax* (*Heteropanax chinensis*) and the mimosa (*Acacia dealbata* 'gauloise') make it feel like this home is inside a forest. A couple of these giants plus several decent-sized plants are enough to create a serious indoor jungle. Make sure you put them in big pots from the outset as repotting them is almost impossible. If the trees grow too large, you can prune them to fit your home.

MICRO AMAZONICA

1 PANDAN OR SCREW PINE
Pandanus utilis

2 REX BEGONIA
Begonia rex

3 PHILODENDRON
Philodendron 'Xanadu'

4 IVY
Hedera hibernica

5 SWISS CHEESE PLANT
Monstera deliciosa

6 LOBSTER CLAW
Heliconia rostrata

7 PHILODENDRON
Philodendron bipinnatifidum

8 EPIPREMNUM
Epipremnum pinnatum

9 SPIDERWORT
Tradescantia zebrina

10 ANTHURIUM
Anthurium

Everywhere in the house, partly due to the rotating walls, you can look out onto the courtyard with its genuine urban jungle. The plants truly have room to grow here. Where the climate is permitting, and the temperature does not get too cold, nor does the air get too dry, many plants that we usually know as houseplants can grow quite enormous. Not limited by a pot, but placed in the open soil, these plants have room for the roots to grow to capacity, supporting more plant growth as well. What grows below the soil will also grow proportionally above the soil. The *Philodendron* (*Philodendron bipinnatifidum*), Swiss cheese plant (*Monstera deliciosa*) and spiderwort (*Tradescantia zebrina*) are thriving here. Even the lobster claw (*Heliconia rostrata*) has grown into a large bush. It is relatively dark in the house, which really suits *Epipremnum* (*Epipremnum pinnatum*). When choosing plants for your indoor areas, take a critical look at the light during the day and choose plants that can grow in such conditions.

VERDANT CHARM

1. **SPIDER PLANT**
   Chlorophytum comosum

2. **DWARF DATE PALM**
   Phoenix roebelenii

3. **ASPARAGUS FERN**
   Asparagus falcatus

4. **CHRISTMAS CACTUS**
   Schlumbergera or Epiphyllum

5. **ELEPHANT'S EAR**
   Alocasia 'Zebrina'

6. **BLUSHWORT**
   Aeschynanthus marmoratus

7. **CHINESE MONEY TREE**
   Crassula ovata

8. **SPURGE**
   Euphorbia pseudocactus

9. **NORFOLK TREE FERN**
   Cyathea brownii

In this neutral interior, clouds of greenery float into view from the constantly growing spider plant (*Chlorophytum comosum*) and the asparagus fern (*Asparagus falcatus*). The palm tree and the hanging plants add to the overall impression, enveloping the house in a bright green haze. Set plants on side tables and little stools, so you can easily move them around and they'll never be in your way.

JUNGLE OF LOVE

1 STAGHORN FERN
Platycerium bifurcatum

2 DIEFFENBACHIA
Dieffenbachia seguine

3 AFRICAN SPEAR
Sansevieria cylindrica

4 BIRD-OF-PARADISE
Strelitzia nicolai

5 SNAKE PLANT
or MOTHER-IN-LAW'S TONGUE
Sansevieria trifasciata

6 FIDDLE-LEAF FIG
Ficus lyrata

7 SPIDERWORT
Tradescantia

8 RUBBER PLANT OR RUBBER FIG
Ficus elastica 'Abidjan' and 'Tineke'

9 SWISS CHEESE PLANT
Monstera deliciosa

10 DWARF TREE FERN
Blechnum gibbum

11 EPIPREMNUM
Epipremnum pinnatum

12 SPIDER PLANT
Chlorophytum comosum

In a house with many big windows and deep windowsills, the possibilities are endless. Provided that they are protected from direct sunlight to some extent, plants can grow into a veritable jungle, which seems to extend into the greenery outside. In the heart of the city, plants grow best in light that comes from a window facing west, north or east. A window facing south is often too light, since direct sunlight can scorch the plants. Anything that grows a bit too quickly can be pruned after a while; you can use those cuttings to grow new plants in water. Plant cuttings from *Scindapsus* (*Scindapsus aureum*), *Epipremnum* (*Epipremnum pinnatum*), spiderwort (*Tradescantia*) and spider plant (*Chlorophytum comosum*) are always excellent choices for growing new plants.

DEPOT BOTANIQUE

1 AFRICAN LINDEN
Sparrmannia africana

2 PENCIL TREE or FIRESTICK PLANT
Euphorbia tirucalli

3 ALOE
Aloe vera

4 SWISS CHEESE PLANT
Monstera deliciosa

5 ROUGH HORSETAIL
Equisetum hyemale

6 MUEHLENBECKIA
Muehlenbeckia complexa

7 SOFT TREE FERN
Dicksonia antarctica

8 FULL MOON MAPLE
Acer japonicum

9 ITALIAN CYPRESS
Cupressus sempervirens

10 BRAZILIAN GIANT RHUBARB
Gunnera manicata

11 DWARF PAPYRUS SEDGE
Cyperus haspans

12 ASPARAGUS FERN
Asparagus setaceus or plumosus

13 FAN PALM
or ROUND LEAF FAN PALM
Livistona rotundifolia

In this former distillery with its wide-open spaces, the indoor plants have a perfect spot due to the bay windows and the light from above. In this loft, plants such as the asparagus fern (*Asparagus setaceus or plumosus*) can literally grow to great heights. Some well-chosen plants in different colours and with different shapes of leaves really give the room an ambiance of its own. The outdoor plants play a significant role in how the green plants in this interior are perceived. Due to the enclosure and the walls of the patio, it seems like an additional indoor space. The green indoors and outdoors are seamlessly integrated as a result. The outdoor plants also have a better chance to grow and survive the cold months on this slightly warmer, sheltered patio.

WUNDERKAMMER

1 ZANZIBAR GEM or ZZ PLANT
Zamioculcas zamiifolia

4 REX BEGONIA
Begonia rex

2 AIR PLANT
Tillandsia oerstediana

5 ORCHID
Phragmipedium

3 ANTHURIUM or LACELEAF
Anthurium spec.

This house is awash in greenery. In Ueli and Florian's home, plants are an intrinsic part of the interior: as objects, highlights and details. There are lovely, exceptional potted plants, but their home also includes cut greens and flower arrangements. It's like being inside a vibrant diorama. The liberal use of striking background colours provides a sharp contrast to the plants in some places and incorporates them ton-sur-ton into the interior in other areas.

PRACTICAL
PLANT INDEX

AFRICA LINDEN or AFRICAN HEMP
(Sparrmannia africana)

ORIGINS	Africa.
WATER	water regularly, keep slightly damp at all times in both summer and winter.
LIGHT	requires a lot of light, but do not place in direct sunlight.
AIR	do not place in too warm a position, and beware of draughts.
CARE	this plant requires a lot of attention, feed occasionally and prune if it gets too big.

AGLAONEMA
(Aglaonema crispum and Aglaonema modestum)

ORIGINS	East Asia, incl. Indonesia, Philippines, Thailand and Sri Lanka.
WATER	it's better to give too little water than too much; irregular watering is not a problem.
LIGHT	can grow with little light, maximum of 2 to 3 hours direct sunlight.
AIR	avoid wide temperature fluctuations, and preferably not too cool.
CARE	grows slowly so it does not need much.
SPECIAL NOTE	excellent air-purifying qualities.

AIRPLANT
(Tillandsia ionanta, filifolia or medusae)

ORIGINS	Central and South America.
WATER	has no roots in the soil, but does need water; mist or soak from time to time.
LIGHT	a light position, but not in direct sunlight.
AIR	will tolerate both low and high temperatures; ensure the environment is not too humid at low temperatures; do not hang near a source of heat.
CARE	mist once or twice a week or immerse in rainwater at room temperature once a week, then leave to drain.

ALOE
(Aloe vera)

ORIGINS	Middle East and North Africa.
WATER	needs little water and the soil can be allowed to dry out between waterings.
LIGHT	can be placed in both partial shade and full sun, but allow the plant to acclimatise.
AIR	tolerates both heat and cold, even below freezing at night.
CARE	requires minimal care.
Special note:	Aloe sap provides relief to wounds and sunburn.

ANTHURIUM or LACELEAF or JUNGLE KING
(Anthurium spec.)

ORIGINS	South America.
WATER	water regularly in small amounts, especially in summer; keep soil slightly damp but not too wet.
LIGHT	place in a bright spot: facing north, or away from the window facing east or west; no direct sunlight.
AIR	needs fairly high humidity, not too low temperatures.
CARE	mist and re-pot occasionally.

ARECA PALM, GOLDEN PALM, YELLOW PALM or BUTTERFLY PALM
(Chrysalidocarpus lutescens)

ORIGINS	tropical Madagascar.
WATER	give small quantities of water on the rootball. and keep the soil slightly damp but not too wet.
LIGHT	requires a lot of light but do not place in direct sunlight.
AIR	enjoys high humidity and conditions that are not too cool.
CARE	mist daily, particularly during the winter months.

ASPARAGUS FERN
(Asparagus setaceus or plumosus)

ORIGINS	South Africa.
WATER	water regularly but do not make the soil too moist.
LIGHT	can cope with a very bright spot, but avoid direct sunlight.
AIR	does well at lower temperatures, do not keep in a warm room to prevent dehydration.
CARE	mist occasionally, re-pot regularly; produces good offshoots.

AUTOGRAPH TREE or PITCH APPLE
(Clusia rosea)

ORIGINS	southern part of the USA, Caribbean and Central America.
WATER	water regularly and allow to dry out a little between waterings.
LIGHT	tolerates a light position, but can also cope with less light and can even be placed in partial shade.
AIR	neither too cold nor too hot.
CARE	requires little care and is a reasonably robust plant.
SPECIAL NOTE	air-purifying plant.

BABY RUBBER PLANT or PEPPER FACE
(Peperomia obtusifolia)

ORIGINS	South America.
WATER	water normally and do not allow to dry out, avoid getting water on the leaves.
LIGHT	place in a light position out of direct sunlight.
AIR	do not place in a cold spot, and beware of draughts.
CARE	easy plant that does not require much special care.

BABY'S TEARS

(Soleirolia soleirolii)

ORIGINS	Mediterranean region, Corsica, Sardinia and the Balearic Islands.
WATER	water regularly and keep slightly damp.
LIGHT	can be placed in a bright spot, but avoid direct sunlight.
AIR	tolerates moderate cold, but also a lot of heat.
CARE	feed occasionally in the summer months.

BAMBOO

(Bambusa vulgaris)

HERKOMST	tropisch en subtropisch Azië.
WATER	heeft veel water nodig.
LICHT	geef hem een lichte plek, maar geen direct zonlicht.
LUCHT	verlangt een hoge luchtvochtigheid dus regelmatig sproeien.
VERZORGING	niet op een plek met tocht of wind zetten.

BAMBOO PALM or BROADLEAF LADY PALM

(Rhapis excelsa)

ORIGINS	Southern China.
WATER	give small amounts of water regularly and keep slightly damp, not wet.
LIGHT	place in a spot that is not too bright and avoid direct sunlight.
AIR	place at room temperature and set outside in summer.
CARE	give plant food occasionally.
SPECIAL NOTE	air-purifying qualities.

BANYAN FIG

(Ficus benghalensis)

ORIGINS	rainforests and mangroves in India.
WATER	water regularly, but do not leave the plant to soak too long.
LIGHT	can be placed in a bright spot, but avoid direct sunlight for longer periods of time.
AIR	tolerates warmer, not too dry spots, and also colder positions, even slight frost.
CARE	fast-growing tree that needs regular feeding.

BIRD-OF-PARADISE

(Strelitzia nicolai and *reginae)*

ORIGINS	South Africa, related to the banana (Musa acuminata).
WATER	water regularly, every day in summer, wetting the leaves; leave the soil damp but not wet.
LIGHT	a position with plenty of light; once acclimatised do not place in direct sunlight for too long.
AIR	will tolerate a reasonably warm spot, not below 10 °C.
CARE	feed once a week and re-pot from time to time.

BIRD'S NEST FERN

(Asplenium nidus)

ORIGINS	Southeast Asia, regions in and around Australia, India and eastern Africa.
WATER	water regularly and keep the soil slightly damp; pour water around the edge of the pot.
LIGHT	can cope with a sunny spot, but does better with less light or by a north-facing window.
AIR	prefers warm, humid air.
CARE	mist regularly, or place in the bathroom.

BLUE STAR FERN

(Phlebodium aureum)

ORIGINS	tropical Asia and the southern regions of North America.
WATER	water regularly, but around the edge of the pot to prevent rot; always keep slightly damp.
LIGHT	pick a semi-shady, slightly sunny spot, not in direct sunlight.
AIR	not too cold; room temperature is fine.
CARE	mist occasionally; this plant is an epiphyte, so ensure that the air roots are not covered by soil.

BOUGAINVILLEA

(Bougainvillea)

ORIGINS	South America, in particular Brazil.
WATER	needs plenty of water and good drainage, do not leave to soak.
LIGHT	needs a pot with plenty of light and hours of sunshine.
AIR	in cooler climates, take the plant inside when colder temperatures are imminent.
CARE	if you want the plant to bloom more, water it less.

BRAZILIAN GIANT RHUBARB or DINOSAUR FOOD

(Gunnera manicata)

ORIGINS	mountain swamps in Brazil and Colombia.
WATER	needs plenty of water and prefers a very humid place in the garden.
LIGHT	can cope with shady areas as well as sunny spots.
AIR	can be planted outdoors in colder climates.
CARE	give plenty of space and cover with straw in winter.

BROMELIA or NEOREGELIA

(Neoregelia)

ORIGINS	Brazil.
WATER	keep soil moist and give water in the flower head and the corners of the tray.
LIGHT	prefers a semi-shaded spot.
AIR	loves high humidity. Do not keep too cold; can be outdoors in slightly warmer climates.
CARE	mist occasionally.

BROMELIA or VRIESEA

(Vriesea fosteriana var. seideliana)

ORIGINS	Brazil.
WATER	make the soil damp occasionally and water the plant through the calyx and axils of the leaves.
LIGHT	prefers a spot with sufficient light, but avoid direct sunlight.
AIR	find a spot that is not too warm and not too cold, but this plant prefers high humidity.
CARE	mist it; after the flowering period, which can last a few months, the plant dies.

BURRO'S TAIL

(Sedum morganianum)

ORIGINS	Mexico and Honduras.
WATER	water generously, but allow the soil to dry out before watering again.
LIGHT	can be placed or hung in a very light place, even in direct sunlight.
AIR	moderate air humidity is good; in mild temperatures, can be placed outdoors.
CARE	give plant food in spring and summer; preferably suspend the plant.

CALADIUM

(Caladium)

ORIGINS	Central and South America, in particular Brazil and the Amazon region.
WATER	keep slightly damp.
LIGHT	does not need much light, moderate light is preferable.
AIR	likes warm, humid conditions, a minimum of 21 °C
CARE	mist plentifully and keep the air humid; difficult houseplant, dies in autumn.

CALATHEA

(Calathea veitchiana)

ORIGINS	Ecuador and Peru.
WATER	water regularly in moderate amounts; do not allow to stand in water.
LIGHT	do not place in bright light; a north-facing window or a position slightly further from the window is advisable.
AIR	does not like rooms that are cool or too warm.
CARE	feed once every two weeks to maintain the leaf colour.

CHERRY LAUREL

(Prunus laurocerasus)

ORIGINS	regions around the Black Sea.
WATER	water regularly but do not allow to stand in water.
LIGHT	prefers partial shade.
AIR	tolerates both heat and cold reasonably well.
CARE	can be pruned in March, June and September.

CHILEAN HARD FERN *(Blechnum chilense)*

ORIGINS	Chile and Argentina.
WATER	needs moist soil.
LIGHT	thrives on low light.
AIR	does require humid air; is able to survive low temperatures.
CARE	mist regularly; can be left in the ground in a temperate climate; grows tall.

CHINESE MONEY TREE

(Crassula ovata)

ORIGINS	South Africa.
WATER	do not give much water; allow the soil to dry out between waterings and do not leave the plant to soak.
LIGHT	when the plant has acclimatised, place in direct sunlight during winter; in summer, reduce the time in direct sunlight.
AIR	prefers fairly dry air and warm temperatures; do not place in a cold spot.
CARE	needs minimal care.

COCONUT TREE

(Cocos nucifera)

ORIGINS	all tropical areas of the Pacific.
WATER	needs plenty of water and good drainage; sometimes needs water as often as twice a day.
LIGHT	needs plenty of light; can even be placed in direct sunlight after an acclimatisation period.
AIR	requires high humidity and must not be placed in a cool area.
CARE	needs a big, deep pot to accommodate its roots; mist plentifully; difficult to keep as a houseplant.

COMMON FIG

(Ficus carica)

ORIGINS	western Asia.
WATER	needs water regularly, especially in summer.
LIGHT	outdoors in a sunny spot.
AIR	may be placed in a moist spot outdoors.
CARE	trim occasionally and add a bit of chalk to the soil.
SPECIAL DETAIL	edible fruit.

CREEPING INCH PLANT

(Callisia repens)

ORIGINS	North America, especially Mexico and Texas.
WATER	give moderate amounts of water and allow the soil to dry out a bit between watering.
LIGHT	can take quite a lot of light, but some shade is also fine.
AIR	not too cool; room temperature is best.
CARE	does not need much care and can be outdoors in summer.

DELTA MAIDENHAIR FERN

(Adiantum raddiamum, venustum and tenerum)

ORIGINS	tropical South America, but also grows in the wild in Europe.
WATER	keep soil slightly damp; give water in small amounts at a time.
LIGHT	thrives on low light, avoid direct sunlight.
AIR	cannot cope with a dry environment or draughts.
CARE	mist regularly to ensure a humid environment.

DESERT CABBAGE

(Kalanchoe NF thyrsiflora)

ORIGINS	Madagascar and South Africa (commonly called *meelplakkie* in South Africa due to the floury white powder on the leaves).
WATER	do not give much water; water every two weeks in summer and even less in winter.
LIGHT	can be placed in a bright spot, even in direct sunlight.
AIR	can be placed in a warm and very dry place with a minimum temperature of 18 °C.
CARE	can be set outside in summer, even in cooler climates, unless it's raining hard.

DIEFFENBACHIA

(Dieffenbachia seguine)

ORIGINS	Brazil and South America.
WATER	keep the soil moist and water regularly; do not leave the plant to soak.
LIGHT	low, preferably filtered light, no direct sunlight.
AIR	requires humid air.
CARE	needs firm support while growing.
IMPORTANT	take care with pets and children.

DRAGON TREE

(Dracaena fragrans)

ORIGINS	Africa, tropical regions in Asia and Central America.
WATER	Provide water when the soil is a bit drier to the touch, do not give too much water or leave the plant to soak.
LIGHT	Can be placed in shadow or in a light spot, but not in direct sunlight.
AIR	Enjoys a pleasant temperature and does not do well in response to major temperature fluctuations.
CARE	Does not need much care; watch out a bit around pets, since the plant is toxic.
SPECIAL DETAIL	Plant has air purifying qualities.

DRAGON TREE

(Dracaena marginata)

ORIGINS	Africa, tropical regions in Asia and Central America.
WATER	provide water when the soil is dry to the touch; do not leave the plant to soak.
LIGHT	does not need much light, thrives in north-facing positions; place colourful Dracaena in a spot with a bit more light.
AIR	preferably not in too cold a spot, prefers room temperature.
CARE	mist occasionally, plant in a large pot if you want to let it grow.

DWARF BANANA

(Musa acuminata 'Super Dwarf Cavendish')

ORIGINS	Southeast Asia.
WATER	give a lot of water in one go, do not allow to stand in water; water more frequently in summer because a lot of moisture evaporates from the leaves.
LIGHT	requires a lot of light; can be placed in direct sunlight, but should be acclimatised gradually.
AIR	mist for higher humidity.
CARE	remove old leaves from the bottom, not the top. Can be placed outdoors in summer.

DWARF PAPYRUS SEDGE

(Cyperus haspans)

ORIGINS	subtropical areas in Africa, Madagascar, South Asia, New Guinea, South America, Central America, southern Mexico, southeast USA.
WATER	needs a lot of water, and you can leave the plant to soak.
LIGHT	can be placed in direct sunlight, but also flourishes in less light.
AIR	quite resilient as a houseplant, provided that the air is not too dry; not hardy in winter.
CARE	occasionally remove dead leaves.

DWARF TREE FERN

(Blechnum gibbum)

ORIGINS	New Caledonia.
WATER	water with soft water or rainwater; always keep the soil damp, but do not leave the plant to soak.
LIGHT	prefers shade to sun.
AIR	avoid temperature fluctuations, and do not place in a position which is too warm in the winter.
CARE	place in a cooler spot in winter and give less water; perfect for the bedroom.

DWARF UMBRELLA TREE or OCTOPUS TREE
(Schefflera arboricola or *Schefflera actinophylla* 'Amante')

ORIGINS	Australia and Taiwan.
WATER	give moderate amounts of water, keep the soil slightly damp in summer and allow the soil to partially dry out in winter.
LIGHT	can be placed in a light or slightly darker area; colourful types require more light; do not overexpose to direct sunlight.
AIR	moderate temperature, not too humid.
CARE	mist and wipe leaves occasionally.

ELEPHANT'S EAR
(Alocasia odora, Alocasia calidora and *Alocasia* 'Zebrina')

ORIGINS	tropical Asia.
WATER	give small amounts of water regularly and keep slightly damp; never allow to dry out completely.
LIGHT	a position with plenty of light; turn regularly to prevent lopsided growth.
AIR	a damp environment at room temperature or slightly warmer.
CARE	re-pot regularly, mist regularly (once or twice a week) and turn occasionally.

ELEPHANT'S FOOT
(Beaucarnea recurvata)

ORIGINS	Central America.
WATER	requires little water because it is stored in the trunk; in winter you need only water once a month.
LIGHT	can be placed in a sunny spot, including a couple of hours in direct sunlight.
AIR:	do not place in too cold a spot: preferably between 10 °C and 18 °C.
CARE	re-pot when the pot gets too small, this stimulates growth.

EPIPREMNUM
(Epipremnum pinnatum, Epipremnum aureum
or *Scindapsus aureum)*

ORIGINS	Southeast Asia and Indonesia.
WATER	give water regularly, do not leave plant to soak; mist or sprinkle with water to rinse dust from the leaves.
LIGHT	can be placed in a bright spot or in a slightly darker area.
AIR	make sure it does not get too cold, or the pattern on the leaves will fade.
CARE	robust plant that thrives on serious pruning.

FALSE SARSAPARILLA
(Hardenbergia violacea)

ORIGINS	Australia and Tasmania.
WATER	water regularly, but don't soak; can also cope with drought.
LIGHT	can be placed in a sunny spot, but also in a slightly shady position.
AIR	can survive a couple of degrees of frost.
CARE	ideal in a conservatory or greenhouse; evergreen.

FALSE SHAMROCK or PURPLE SHAMROCK
(Oxalis triangularis)

ORIGINS	Brazil.
WATER	keep slightly damp.
LIGHT	becomes most attractive and flowers most beautifully with plenty of light, but avoid direct sunlight.
AIR	does not require high humidity.
CARE	requires little care and can be placed outdoors in summer.
Special note:	edible plant provided you have grown it yourself or have bought it as an edible plant.

FAN PALM or ROUND LEAF FAN PALM
(Livistona rotundifolia)

ORIGINS	tropical open forests in Asia and Northern Australia.
WATER	requires small amounts of water several times a week.
LIGHT	can cope with plenty of light as well as a more shady spot; avoid direct sunlight.
AIR	do not place in too cold a spot and do not expose to temperatures below 20 °C for too long.
CARE	give rainwater and place outside in summer; mist in winter to prevent dehydration.

FICUS TREE or WEEPING FIG
(Ficus benjamina)

ORIGINS	South Asia, Southeast Asia and Australia.
WATER	keep soil slightly damp and give water in small amounts at a time.
LIGHT	requires plenty of light, including several hours of direct sunlight.
AIR	avoid low temperatures and keep the humidity high.
CARE	sprinkle with water regularly, once a week in summer, twice a week in winter.

FIDDLE-LEAF FIG
(Ficus lyrata)

ORIGINS	rainforests in Africa.
WATER	regularly water around the edge of the pot, not onto the roots; keep moist to prevent dehydration.
LIGHT	thrives in both brighter and shadier spots; when placed in an area with less light, the plant needs less water.
AIR	not too cold and keep the air humid.
CARE	mist regularly.

FISHTAIL PALM or TODDY PALM

(Caryota mitis)

ORIGINS	Indonesia and Malaysia.
WATER	requires generous amounts of lukewarm water, but preferably a lot in one go rather than small amounts more frequently.
LIGHT	does not need a bright spot; a spot with low light will also suffice, but the amount of light will influence the colour.
AIR	does not require high humidity and can also be placed in a cooler spot.
CARE	can grow big and have deep roots; occasional re-potting into a bigger pot recommended.

FLOWERING IVY or CAPE IVY or NATAL IVY

(Senecio macroglossus)

ORIGINS	Southern and south-eastern Africa.
WATER	Water regularly; keep soil slightly damp, but don't let it get too wet.
LIGHT	Can handle lots of light, as well as direct sunlight.
AIR	Semi-hardy in winter.
CARE	Low-maintenance.

FULL MOON MAPLE

(Acer japonicum)

ORIGINS	Japan.
WATER	keep the soil in the pot slightly damp; add water when the temperature is high.
LIGHT	can be placed in a shady area with low light.
AIR	can cope with an extremely cold environment.
CARE	do not place in a windy area; can also be placed in pots on a patio.

**HAIRY STEMMED RHIPSALIS
or HAIRY-FRUITED WICKERWARE CACTUS**

(Rhipsalis pilocarpa)

ORIGINS	Central and South America.
WATER	do not give much water.
LIGHT	can cope with low light, a north-facing window would be a good spot.
AIR	do not place in a humid area, but keep cool and dry.
CARE	trim off the occasional brown and yellow leaves; does not require plant food; slow-growing.

HART'S-TONGUE FERN

(Asplenium scolopendrium)

ORIGINS	parts of Europe, northern Africa, North America, Asia and Japan.
WATER	water regularly and keep slightly damp.
LIGHT	thrives on low light, away from the window, or north-facing.
AIR	does well in the living room, as long as it's not too dry.
CARE	mist regularly, or place in the bathroom for a while.

HEDGE CACTUS or QUEEN OF THE NIGHT

(Cereus hildmannianus)

ORIGINS	South America, Brazil, Paraguay, Uruguay and Argentina.
WATER	give small quantities of water and allow the soil to dry out between waterings.
LIGHT	will tolerate a lot of light, including direct sunlight.
AIR	can cope with both cold (below freezing) and heat.
CARE	little care required, re-pot from time to time.

ITALIAN CYPRESS

(Cupressus sempervirens)

ORIGINS	Mediterranean region.
WATER	in very dry, warm weather, give the plant a bit more water.
LIGHT	can cope with light or semi-shade.
AIR	tolerates both very dry air and humid air very well.
CARE	preferably plant in the ground outdoors; needs little care and can be pruned to keep it compact.
SPECIAL NOTE	evergreen.

IVY

(Hedera hibernica)

ORIGINS	Atlantic coasts of Europe.
WATER	water regularly in pots and containers.
LIGHT	can be placed in shade, partial shade or sun.
AIR	will withstand moderately cold conditions, but is not entirely hardy in northern Europe.
CARE	cover pots in winter, prune in March/April.

JAPANESE ARALIA or GLOSSY-LEAVED PAPER PLANT

(Fatsia japonica)

ORIGINS	Japan.
Water:	does not need watering very often, but give a lot of water in one go.
LIGHT	can be placed in dark places indoors, in partial shade or full shade.
AIR	can be placed in a cool spot, outdoors down to -10 °C; needs moderate humidity.
CARE	a robust and easy plant, handy if you're away often.

KENTIA PALM or THATCH PALM

(Howea forsteriana)

ORIGINS	islands off Australia.
WATER	water regularly and keep the soil constantly moist but not too wet; do not let the soil dry out.
LIGHT	can be placed in a light or slightly darker area, but not in direct sunlight.
AIR	ensure the environment is not too dry and keep at room temperature; if necessary, mist the plant for humidity.

CARE   if the leaves turn yellow, move the palm closer to the window; occasionally re-pot in spring.

LIPSTICK PLANT
(*Aeschynanthus* and *Aeschynanthus 'Twister'*)

ORIGINS	humid forests in Asia.
WATER	water regularly and do not let the soil dry out.
LIGHT	thrives on low light, preferably out of direct sunlight.
AIR	not too cool or in a draught.
CARE	set in a cooler spot in winter to encourage flower buds to form.

LOBSTER CLAW
(*Heliconia rostrata*)

ORIGINS	South America.
WATER	needs regular watering, but avoid pouring water onto the roots.
LIGHT	needs a lot of light, preferably filtered light.
AIR	needs a fairly warm, humid environment.
CARE	needs feeding from time to time.
SPECIAL NOTE	pollinated by birds such as the hummingbird.

MACHO FERN
(*Nephrolepis exaltata*)

ORIGINS	New Zealand and tropical Asia.
WATER	water regularly; keep soil moist.
LIGHT	tolerates low light; can even thrive in shadier spots.
AIR	does well at room temperature, can cope with slightly drier air occasionally.
CARE	thin out and re-pot regularly.

MALABAR CHESTNUT or MONEY TREE
(*Pachira aquatica*)

ORIGINS	Brazil, Panama and Costa Rica.
WATER	water generously from time to time and allow the trunk to take up the water in between; give slightly more water in summer than in winter.
LIGHT	light position, but no direct sunlight; the leaves will fade if placed in a north-facing position or too far from the window.

MARANTA or CALATHEA
(*Calathea zebrina*)

ORIGINS	South America.
WATER	water regularly and keep slightly damp.
LIGHT	can be placed in a bright spot, but preferably avoid direct sunlight.
AIR	needs humid air.
CARE	mist with lukewarm water, does not need much plant food and is fairly robust. Special note: the plant curls up its leaves at night or when it gets warm.

MEXICAN SNOWBALL
(*Echeveria elegans*)

ORIGINS	Mexico.
WATER	do not give much water and allow the soil to dry out between waterings; provide more water in summer.
LIGHT	tolerates plenty of sunlight, but also does fine in less light.
AIR	can cope with heat, but also does fine in lower temperatures.
CARE	needs minimal care, can be set outside on the deck or patio in summer; in case of heavy rainfall, place it under shelter.

MISTLETOE CACTUS or RHIPSALIS
(*Rhipsalis cassutha* or *baccifera*)

ORIGINS	South America and tropical Africa.
WATER	water moderately and allow to dry out slightly between waterings.
LIGHT	will grow well in reduced light.
AIR	prefers air that it not too dry at room temperature.
CARE	requires minimal care.

MOTHER-IN-LAW'S CUSHION
(*Echinocactus grusonii*)

ORIGINS	Mexico.
WATER	do not give much water and allow the soil to dry out between waterings.
LIGHT	prefers a bright spot and will tolerate direct sunlight.
AIR	dry air is not a problem; can also cope with lower or higher temperatures.
CARE	requires very little care, does not need much water.

MOTHER-IN-LAW'S TONGUE
(*Sansevieria trifasciata* or *snakeplant*)

ORIGINS	tropical western Africa.
WATER	do not give much water and allow the soil to dry out between waterings.
LIGHT	can cope with plenty of light, but no direct sunlight.
AIR	room temperature and not too cold.
CARE	does not thrive in a pot that's too large.

MUEHLENBECKIA
(*Muehlenbeckia*)

ORIGINS	mountainous regions of New Zealand.
WATER	water regularly and do not let the soil dry out; the warmer it gets, the more you need to water it.
LIGHT	preferably semi-shade or bright light, can also cope with direct sunlight.
AIR	not too dry.

CARE   can be placed indoors or outdoors, at temperatures as low as -5 °C or even -20 °C depending on species; give plant food occasionally.

NORFOLK ISLAND PINE
(Araucaria heterophylla)
ORIGINS   Norfolk Island off Australia.
WATER   water regularly and keep slightly damp, do not leave to stand in water.
LIGHT   grows well in partial shade.
AIR   do not place in too cold a position; can also be placed outdoors in warmer regions.
CARE   feed regularly in spring and summer, prune off dead branches.

OLIVE TREE
(Olea europaea)
ORIGINS   Southern Europe and North Africa.
WATER   requires plenty of water on a regular basis; allow to partly dry out.
LIGHT   needs a lot of direct sunlight, particularly in spring; not too close to the window.
AIR   watch out for draughts.
CARE   plant in good, well draining clay soil; can be placed indoors or outdoors.

ORCHID
(Cymbidium)
ORIGINS   Asia (Nepal, Vietnam, Taiwan, Himalayas) and Australia.
WATER   do not give much water; allow the soil to dry out between waterings.
LIGHT   preferably place in a bright spot, but not in direct sunlight.
AIR   can be placed outdoors in mild temperatures.
CARE   mist buds that have yet to bloom; after the flowering period, cut off the stem at the bottom.

PARLOUR PALM
(Chamaedorea elegans)
ORIGINS   rainforests of southern Mexico and Guatemala.
WATER   water regularly and keep slightly damp, do not allow to dry out.
LIGHT   can be placed in both partial shade and partial sun.
AIR   does not require high humidity and can happily be placed in a dry living room.
CARE   mist and regularly check for red spider mite.

PEACE LILY
(Spathiphyllum and Spathiphyllum 'Sensation')
ORIGINS   Colombia and Venezuela.
WATER   keep the soil moist, can cope with a large amount of water all at once; may occasionally be soaked.

LIGHT   can be placed in a moderately light position or even a spot with minimal light.
AIR   in warmer climates, can be kept outside, in pots or in the ground.
CARE   give plant food occasionally; after the flowering period, cut off the flower stem and flyleaf stem completely.
SPECIAL NOTE   air-purifying qualities.

PENCIL TREE or FIRESTICK PLANT
(Euphorbia tirucalli)
ORIGINS   southern and eastern Africa.
WATER   do not give much water.
LIGHT   place in a bright spot.
AIR   can cope with dry conditions.
CARE   requires minimal care; will tolerate cooler temperatures in winter.

PERUVIAN APPLE CACTUS
(Cereus peruvianus)
ORIGINS   Peru.
WATER   do not give much water and allow the soil to dry out between waterings.
LIGHT   prefers a bright spot and can cope with direct sunlight.
AIR   dry air as well as lower or higher temperatures are not a problem.
CARE   requires very minimal care, does not need much water.

PHILODENDRON
(Philodendron 'Imperial Red')
ORIGINS   Central and South America.
WATER   water regularly and keep slightly damp, do not give too much water in one go.
LIGHT   prefers indirect light or a position with low light.
AIR   do not place in too cold a spot and ensure high humidity.
CARE   mist regularly.

PHILODENDRON
(Philodendron martianum)
ORIGINS   rainforests in southeast Brazil.
WATER   water regularly in small amounts, may be kept slightly damp but not wet.
LIGHT   thrives on low light.
AIR   do not place in too cold a spot; can be placed outdoors in warmer areas.
CARE   preferably give rainwater, tap water contains too many salts; mist occasionally; grows better in a large pot.

PHILODENDRON
(Philodendron scandens)

ORIGINS	South American rainforests.
WATER	water regularly in small amounts and keep the soil slightly damp.
LIGHT	can cope with low light, preferably avoiding direct sunlight.
AIR	prefers humid air that is not too cold.
CARE	mist frequently, including the aerial roots.

PHILODENDRON
(Philodendron selloum or Philodendron bipinnatifidum)

ORIGINS	South American rainforests.
WATER	keep soil slightly damp and do not give too much water at once.
LIGHT	thrives on low light, absolutely no direct sunlight.
AIR	enjoys high humidity.
CARE	in winter, check that it is not too dry, and don't forget to mist.

PHILODENDRON
(Philodendron squamiferum)

ORIGINS	North Brazil and Surinam.
WATER	regularly needs small amounts of water; can cope with occasionally skipping watering.
LIGHT	thrives on low light, but will tolerate a little sunlight.
AIR	can cope with high air humidity.
CARE	a regular sprinkling of water is good.

PHILODENDRON
(Philodendron 'Xanadu')

ORIGINS	mainly South America.
WATER	keep soil moist, but not too wet – regularly give water in small amounts.
LIGHT	thrives on low light; avoid direct sunlight.
AIR	do not place in a very cool or cold spot.
CARE	occasionally re-pot young plants in spring; give plant food in moderate amounts.

PITCHER PLANT
(Sarrascenia)

ORIGINS	eastern coastal regions of North America and southern Canada.
WATER	needs plenty of water and humidity and slightly acidic soil.
LIGHT	bright and sunny during the growing period, less light in the resting period in winter.
AIR	preferably a humid environment, to avoid dehydrating the pitcher.
CARE	give rainwater or distilled water.

PRAYER PLANT
(Maranta leuconeura)

ORIGINS	tropical rainforests in South America.
WATER	always keep the soil slightly damp, but do not leave the plant to soak; make sure the water is not too cold.
LIGHT	requires a bright spot, but avoid direct sunlight; in a bright spot, the plant will retain its colouring.
AIR	requires high humidity.
CARE	mist regularly.

REX BEGONIA AND LEAF BEGONIA
(Begonia rex and Begonia mazae)

ORIGINS	Mexico.
WATER	give small quantities of lukewarm water regularly, do not allow soil to dry out. Ensure good drainage.
LIGHT	can be in relatively light spot, but semi-shaded is also fine; no direct sun.
AIR	do not put somewhere too warm or too dry.
CARE	do not mist.

RHIPSALIS or RED MISTLETOE CACTUS
(Rhipsalis ramulosa 'Red Coral' and Rhipsalis baccifera)

ORIGINS	South and Central America and Florida.
WATER	give moderate or small amounts of water; allow the soil to dry out between waterings.
LIGHT	can be hung in a spot with plenty of light or a little less light.
AIR	able to survive low temperatures, from just above 0 °C up to around 35 °C.
CARE	give plant food regularly.
SPECIAL NOTE	if exposed to plenty of light, the leaf tips turn a lovely red.

ROUGH HORSETAIL
(Equisetum hyemale)

ORIGINS	Eurasia and North America.
WATER	requires plenty of water; as an outdoor plant, it does better when planted in the ground.
LIGHT	can cope with a semi-shaded spot as well as with plenty of sunlight.
AIR	able to withstand extremely cold temperatures, down to -29 °C.
CARE	plant in pots in the ground to prevent it from running rampant.

RUBBER FIG
(Ficus elastica 'Abidjan' or 'Tineke')

ORIGINS	Central and South America, Southeast Asia and Australia.
WATER	give moderate amounts of water, do not keep soil very wet or leave the plant to soak.
LIGHT	indirect light; either a light or shady spot, but avoid direct sunlight.
AIR	do not place in a draught; temperatures above 15 °C.

CARE   wipe leaves occasionally.

SCHLUMBERGERA or CHRISTMAS CACTUS
(Schlumbergera, also Epiphyllum)

ORIGINS	mountains of Central and South America.
WATER	water moderately.
LIGHT	plenty of light, but no direct sunlight.
AIR	room temperature, outdoors in summer.
CARE	requires little care, easy to propagate.

SCINDAPSUS
(Scindapsus pictus)

ORIGINS	Bangladesh, Thailand, Malaysia and Indonesian islands.
WATER	water regularly, do not leave standing in water; mist or spray to remove dust from the leaves.
LIGHT	can tolerate both bright spots and a position with reduced light.
AIR	not too cold, otherwise the leaf markings will fade.
CARE	robust plant that can be vigorously pruned.

SCREW PINE or PANDAN
(Pandanus utilis)

ORIGINS	island coasts in the Pacific Ocean.
WATER	keep slightly damp in the winter, water moderately during the growing period in the summer and allow the soil to dry out slightly between waterings.
LIGHT	can be placed in a light position, but preferably not in direct sunlight.
AIR	enjoys high humidity.
CARE	mist and feed occasionally.

SENTRY PLANT or 100-YEAR-OLD-ALOE
(Agave americana)

ORIGINS	dry regions in Mexico and Central America.
WATER	give small amounts of water and allow to dry out thoroughly, particularly in the winter.
LIGHT	light position, tolerates direct sunlight.
AIR	can cope with very dry, warm air.
CARE	can be placed outdoors in the summer at temperatures above 5 °C.

SKELETON PLANT or ALOCASIA
(Alocasia amazonica and Alocasia zebrina)

ORIGINS	tropical Asia.
WATER	give small amounts of water regularly and keep slightly damp; never allow to dry out completely.
LIGHT	a position with plenty of light; turn regularly to prevent lopsided growth.
AIR	a humid environment at room temperature or slightly warmer.
CARE	re-pot regularly, mist regularly (once or twice a week) and turn occasionally.

SICKLETHORN
(Asparagus falcatus)

ORIGINS	South Africa.
WATER	water moderately and allow the soil to dry out a bit in between.
LIGHT	lots of light, no direct sun.
AIR	prefers humid air - not too warm or too dry.
CARE	mist regularly, re-pot periodically.

SOFT TREE FERN
(Dicksonia antarctica)

ORIGINS	Australia and Tasmania.
WATER	water regularly and keep the crown and stem damp.
LIGHT	can cope with shady as well as sunny spots.
AIR	can withstand cold temperatures outdoors, but when the temperature drops below 5 °C, ensure that the crown and stem remain moist.
CARE	feed occasionally; below -10 °C, protect the plant with a cover and plant the pot in the ground.

SPIDER ALOE
(Aloe vera spinosissima)

ORIGINS	South Africa to tropical Africa and the surrounding islands.
WATER	do not give much water; water every two weeks in summer and even less in winter.
LIGHT	can be placed in a bright spot, even in direct sunlight.
AIR	an arid environment is not a problem; keep the temperature above 15 °C.
CARE	needs minimal care, but occasional feeding is good for the aloe; can be set outside in summer, even in cooler climates.

SPIDER PLANT
(Chlorophytum comosum)

ORIGINS	Africa and Asia.
WATER	water regularly and keep slightly damp.
LIGHT	a bright spot, but not in direct sunlight.
AIR	not too cold or too dry, not in a draught; mist occasionally.
CARE	does not need much plant food; new offshoots can be replanted or allowed to continue growing as a trailing plant.

SPIDERWORT
(Tradescantia and Tradescantia zebrina)

ORIGINS	tropical rainforests in Asia.
WATER	water regularly; do not let the soil dry out.
LIGHT	can be kept at room temperature.
AIR	moderately humid, not too dry.
CARE	mist occasionally; plant can produce lovely blossoms.

SPINELESS YUCCA

(Yucca elephantipes)

ORIGINS	dry regions in North and South America and the Caribbean.
WATER	do not give too much water, particularly avoid over-watering in winter and allow to partially dry out.
LIGHT	prefers a bright spot, even with some direct sunlight.
AIR	does not require high humidity at room temperature.
CARE	re-pot in spring and only feed occasionally in spring and summer.

STAGHORN FERN

(Platycerium bifurcatum)

ORIGINS	tropical jungles in Australia.
WATER	water regularly (preferably with rainwater) or soak, and keep soil moist.
LIGHT	shade or semi-shade, absolutely no direct sunlight.
AIR	can cope with warm rooms.
CARE	do not wipe off the white, waxy layer.

SWISS CHEESE PLANT

(Monstera deliciosa)

ORIGINS	tropical rainforests in South America.
WATER	give water regularly, but do not oversaturate the soil; give more water in summer to compensate for evaporation, and far less water in winter.
LIGHT	partial shade, some light but no direct sunlight; do not move the plant around
AIR	room temperature, not below 10 °C; mist regularly.
CARE	robust plant; the aerial roots (floating roots) can be trimmed off or guided towards the soil.

SYNGONIUM

(Syngonium podophyllum)

ORIGINS	Latin America, Mexico and Bolivia.
WATER	water regularly , but do not allow to stand in water.
LIGHT	does not need much light.
AIR	do not place in too cool a spot; can survive in dry air but grows better with some humidity.
CARE	mist occasionally.

TAILFLOWER

(Anthurium andraeanum)

ORIGINS	Colombia and Ecuador, Venezuela, the Antilles and the Windward Islands.
WATER	give a little water regularly and keep slightly damp; water less in winter.
LIGHT	requires a light position, but no direct sunlight; will also tolerate partial shade, but will then bloom less and be slower to come into flower.
AIR	requires high humidity; do not place in too cold a spot, and preferably keep at a constant temperature.

TRIANGLE CACTUS

(Acanthocereus tetragonus)

ORIGINS	southern North America, Central America and northern South America.
WATER	do not give too much water, and allow the soil to dry out.
LIGHT	can acclimatise to direct sunlight.
AIR	will tolerate wide fluctuations in temperature.
CARE	requires little care.

TROPICAL FERN

(Nephrolepis biserrata)

ORIGINS	Florida, Mexico, South America and the West Indies.
WATER	water regularly and keep soil damp.
LIGHT	can do with less light.
AIR	loves humid conditions.
CARE	mist regularly, divide and report occasionally.

UMBRELLA BAMBOO

(Fargesia murieliae)

ORIGINS	China.
WATER	give ample water regularly, especially if the bamboo is potted.
LIGHT	can be in direct sunlight, but shade is also fine.
AIR	very hard, can stay outdoors on the terrace all winter.
CARE	does not need much care.
SPECIAL DETAIL	evergreen, quick-growing, non-proliferating type of bamboo.

WAX PLANT

(Hoya carnosa or Hoya carnosa compacta)

ORIGINS	India, China and Australia.
WATER	water occasionally and allow to dry out between waterings.
LIGHT	needs moderate or bright light, but no direct sunlight.
AIR	room temperature and humid air.
CARE	mist regularly; leave wilted flowers in place.

ZAMIOCULCAS or ZANZIBAR GEM

(Zamioculcas zamiifolia)

ORIGINS	Central Africa; Kenya and Zanzibar.
WATER	give moderate amounts of water, especially during cooler weather.
LIGHT	place in a bright spot, but avoid direct sunlight.
AIR	can always cope with a warm spot, even in winter.
CARE	needs minimal care; treat like a succulent.

LIST VOC
(VOLATILE ORGANIC COMPOUNDS)

ACETONE

is found e.g. in: cosmetics and nail polish remover, air fresheners and cleaning products.

ALCOHOL

is found e.g. in: wallpaper, cosmetics, drywall and particle board, glue, air fresheners, paint, varnish and flooring.

AMMONIA

is found e.g. in: cleaning products, printers and copy machines.

BENZENE

is found e.g. in: pesticides, drywall, inks and dyes, glue, petroleum products, plastics, tobacco smoke, rubber products, particle board, synthetics, flooring and wallpaper.

FORMALDEHYDE

is found e.g. in: furniture upholstery, cosmetics, facial wipes, drywall, compressed wood and wood board, curtain fabrics, insulation material, air fresheners, paper towels, plastic bags and trash bags, cleaning products, plywood, paint, varnish and flooring.

TRICHLOROETHYLENE

is found e.g. in: stain, ink, polish, glue, dry-cleaning chemicals, paint and varnish.

XYLEEN

is found e.g. in: wallpaper, drywall and particle board, glue, printers and copy machines, paint, varnish and flooring.

PLANT INDEX

GLOSSARY

ASSIMILATION

this is the process in the chloroplasts in the leaves through which photosynthesis converts CO_2 and water into glucose and other by-products. A plant uses these elements to grow.

INDOOR PLANT

this is a plant that we brought back from a warmer climate, which we can keep indoors in cooler climates. Also known as a houseplant.

WIPING LEAVES

dusting smooth (non-fuzzy) leaves with a damp cloth.

BRIGHTLY COLOURED LEAVES

leaves that have a coloured pattern due to genetic defects in e.g. cell structures or pigment concentration.

OUTDOOR PLANT

plant that can thrive outside in a pot or in the ground in the local climate.

DRAINAGE

options for draining water from the soil.

DRY AIR

air that has low humidity. In living rooms that have an active heating system or in desert regions.

DRY OUT

let the soil dry out completely.

HANGING PLANT

plant suitable to grow downwards from an elevated location.

ROOM TEMPERATURE

15 °C - 21 °C.

KOKEDAMA

Japanese decorative botanical art form in which a plant or tree is kept artificially small by wrapping it in moss. These 'balls of moss' are attached free-floating to the ceiling.

AIR HUMIDITY

the amount of moisture/water in the air.

AERIAL ROOTS

roots above the ground, which grow into the air. Plants often use these to attach themselves to trees to climb upwards.

MIST

spray the plants with water using a fine-spray bottle.

POTTING SOIL

dirt in a specific composition that's good for plants, usually combining a mixture of different types of soil, such as peat litter, peat moss, coconut fibre, lava stones and clay. Generic indoor potting soil is generally fine for houseplants, but some plants do better in special soil designed especially for succulents or orchids.

ELONGATE

in a case of insufficient light, the stems of a plant stretch out, and the plant produces less foliage.

PRUNE

use a sharp, clean knife or pruning shears to remove branches and stems that grow too long.

CUTTING

a technique for breeding plants by replanting a part of the parent plant. For instance, a leaf or stem.

RUNNER OR OFFSHOOT

young stem with leaves and shoots that has recenty grown.

DEHYDRATE

let the soil dry out completely.

RE-POT

move a plant into a larger pot and/or give it new potting soil.

HUMID AIR

air with a high humidity level, as in conservatories or tropical regions.

OPEN GROUND

soil without divisions or limits, such as in a garden or very large planter.

IRRIGATION SYSTEM

automatic or semi-automatic watering system.

ROOT ROT

a plant's roots rot because they are affected by soil fungus (Phytophthora) due to the soil being too wet.

STRETCHING

The plant's stems will grow longer and the spaces between the leaves will increase. The plant will often reduce the amount of foliage.

This book is
MARKED

MARKED is an initiative by Lannoo Publishers.
www.markedbylannoo.com

JOIN THE MARKED COMMUNITY
 @markedbylannoo

Or sign up for our MARKED newsletter with news about new and forthcoming publications on art, interior design, food & travel, photography and fashion as well as exclusive offers and MARKED events on www.markedbylannoo.com

Text interiors: Irene Schampaert
Text plants: Judith Baehner
Image editing: Irene Schampaert
Translation: Joy Phillips
Copy-editing: Robert Fulton
Book design: Irene Schampaert
Illustrations: Georgina Taylor & Maaike Koster
Cover image: Rebenque

If you have any questions or comments about the material in this book, please do not hesitate to contact our editorial team: markedteam@lannoo.com.

© Lannoo Publishers, Belgium, 2020
D/2020/45/449 – NUR 422/454
9789401472050
2nd print run

#AREYOUMARKED

PHOTO CREDITS

008 **WABI-SABI** STOCKHOLM I SE
© Anna Malmberg
(www.annamalmbergphoto.com) www.fantasticfrank.se

019 **CINEMA FLORA** CREMONA I IT
© Maria Teresa Furnari

028 **GREEN, GREY & GLAMOROUS** ANTWERP I BE
© Yannick Milpas

040 **ASIAN DREAM** CHAU DOC I VN
© Nishizawaarchitects

050 **PARIS TEXAS** ANTWERP I BE
© Tim Van de Velde

062 **OFICIO STUDIO** MADRID I ES
© www.rebenque.com

072 **GREEN DIY DREAM** MELBOURNE I AU
© Annette O'Brien for The Design Files

081 **SCANDINAVIAN IMMACULACY** COPENHAGEN DK
© Photographer: Christina Onsgaard Kayser / IDECORimages.
Stylist: Rikke Graff Juel / IDECORimages.

088 **FRENCH GRANDEUR** PARIS I FR
© Birgitta Wolfgang / Sisters Agency

098 **GREEN STATEMENTS** MILAN I IT
© Serge Anton

107 **INDOOR PATIO** AVARE I BR
© Pedro Kok

116 **BOTANIC ELEGANCE** GHENT I BE
© Stefanie Faveere

127 **PASTEL PERFECT** LA I US
© Marisa Vitale

137 **GARDEN HOUSE** TOKYO I JP
© Iwan Baan

143 **ATELIER ARTISTIQUE** MADRID I ES
© Belén Imaz (photography) / Pete Bermejo (styling)

150 **EXOTIC EYE CATCHERS** BOSTON I US
© Emily Billings

159 **PRET-A-PORTER** PHILADELPHIA I US
© Carina Romano / Apartment Therapy

167 **LOFT CINEMATIC** MADRID I ES
© Gonzalo Machado

174 **URBAN GREEN** NEW YORK I US
© Erica Gannett

183 **INDOOR JUNGLE** LIER I BE
© Jan Verlinde

191 **MICRO AMAZONICA** MARINGA I BR
© Bulla Jr Photo

198 **VERDANT CHARM** BENTVELD I NL
© Anouk De Kleermaeker

209 **JUNGLE OF LOVE** BALTIMORE US
© Hilton Carter

218 **DEPOT BOTANIQUE** ANTWERP I BE
© Verne Photography

229 **WUNDERKAMMER** AMSTERDAM NL
© James Stokes